NOT A MATCH

My True Tales of Online Dating Disasters

BRIAN DONOVAN

Thought Catalog Books
Brooklyn, NY

THOUGHT CATALOG BOOKS

Copyright © 2015 by Brian Donovan

All rights reserved. Published by Thought Catalog Books, a division of The Thought & Expression Co., Williamsburg, Brooklyn. For general information and submissions: manuscripts@thoughtcatalog.com.

First edition, 2015
ISBN 978-0692577820
10 9 8 7 6 5 4 3 2 1

Founded in 2010, Thought Catalog is a website and imprint dedicated to your ideas and stories. We publish fiction and non-fiction from emerging and established writers across all genres.

Cover image by © iStock.com/Spiderstock

CONTENTS

WHY, OH WHY, AM I WRITING THIS BOOK?!

I have been out on dates, friends, and they have come from the Internet. I've been on dates with doctors and nurses, students and teachers, athletes and academics. I've been out with black women, white women, short women, tall women, women who I'm not even sure were women at all. I have met long-term girlfriends, and friends I'll keep for years. I've also met women who, if I saw them on the street, I would sprint–not run, mind you, but sprint--in the opposite direction. Why am I telling you this? To explain why I'm writing this book.

Several years and over 100 dates ago, I decided to give Internet dating a try. (Wow. 100 Internet dates. It's kind of humiliating when I write it out like that. In fact, this is all kind of humiliating. Is it too late to stop writing?) I was hoping to find, quite simply, a solid, long-term relationship. A great woman who made me laugh, think, and generally want to high five everyone in the world.

And, to be fair, I have met a few girls that are worthy of high-fives, but along with them came a whole lot of low fives. Very low fives. Fours, even. Girls who cried, girls who lied, girls who made fun of me on national TV. And that is why we are gathered here today. Because if I went out on all those ridiculous dates just to find a few promising women, well...Good Lord was that a waste of time. But if I can pass these stories on to you so that you may learn from, or at the very least, laugh at my mistakes, then it'll all be worth it. OK, it won't be even close to worth it, but I need something to tell myself before the crying and the panic sweat starts.

It took me several crazy encounters before I realized that I should probably start writing this nonsense down. It came to me on a date that started the way many Internet dates do: with a person who looked nothing like her pictures. I had met up with a woman who online looked like Jessica Biel, but in person was a lot closer to Jessica Tandy. Honestly, I looked as much like this woman's photos as she did. But for me, it wasn't a deal breaker. I was searching for something of substance, something more than skin deep. So what if she wasn't perfect? I'm not perfect. In fact, Perfect takes one look at me, laughs, then texts her friends a picture so they can get a gander at this insanely imperfect guy she just met. So once I got past the whole foundation-built-on-lies thing,

I decided to stick it out. Because what initially attracted me to Annie was not her appearance, but what she did for a living.

Annie taught deaf children, you see, and described it as the defining experience of her life. Her profile spoke eloquently about the challenges she faced everyday, and how she never imagined that this was where her life would lead. Now that was a girl I had to know. Someone willing to do something so difficult, so unconventional––it really caught my eye. I have a thing for quirk, for people who do the unexpected (for evidence of this assertion, see every subsequent page of this book), and if she taught deaf children she had to be, at the very least, really nice, right? Even though she fudged a bit about how she looked, clearly Annie was someone with an interesting story to tell. So I bided my time, then, after the first drink, I went for the heart…

Me: So how did you get into teaching deaf children? That must be so challenging, and just an amazing–

Annie: Oh, I didn't want to really. But it costs less to get a degree in teaching the deaf than it does to teach normal kids, so I figured, "why not?

Me (mulling over "normal" as a word choice): …Oh? Do they give out grants or something?

Annie: Yeah, and now I know why. It sucks. The thing about deaf kids is that they can't hear you, like, at all. It gets really frustrating. Sometimes I just kinda give up.

Me: That seems…wait, you give up?

Annie: Well, yelling doesn't work because they're deaf, you know? They don't really prepare you for that in the classes.

Me (looking around to see if anyone else is getting this): Yeah, no that must be-

Annie: But I'm just doing it to save up money. My first love is blackjack.

Me: Blackjack?

Annie: Yeah, I go down to Atlantic City every Friday and play through the weekend. When I save up enough I'm gonna quit teaching and become a professional blackjack player. Gambling is so much more fun than teaching deaf children. And you're allowed to drink.

And that's when I started looking around for a fire alarm, hoping that maybe I could shake her in all the commotion. Sure, I was searching for unconventional, but a teacher who was killing time with the disabled until she could hit AC? That was a bit much, even for me. I was frustrated, tired, and regretting the day I ever typed Match.com into my Google machine. I could've left then, but Annie and I both had full drinks in front of us, so I figured, "what's another 15 minutes?" That's when I asked her the one question I had left in my arsenal, and got the idea that ultimately lead to this book. "So Annie," I said optimistically, "tell me about the worst Internet date you've ever been on." This was her answer...

"A few months back, I went out with an investment banker," Annie told me, and immediately I knew we were onto something. Investment bankers are, as everyone knows, douche bags. It's one of the universal laws of our planet. They're entitled, they all wear exactly the same clothes all the time, and were all seemingly born with a drinking problem. If anyone was gonna act like a dick on a first date, it was an I-Banker. And, to top it all off, he'd asked Annie out to dinner. NEVER go out to dinner on a first date. It takes too damn long, and if you figure out you've got a jerk on your hands during the appetizer, you're pretty much locked in until after dessert. And jerks always order dessert. But actually, Annie said, he was quite pleasant through the salad course and seemed fairly promising halfway through the entrees. Until...

JP, we'll call him, because those guys are always named JP, had had too many drinks. He held his liquor fairly well because, as noted earlier, he'd been drinking since birth––but apparently it was beginning to show. He drank expensive vodka on the rocks, as dictated by the Douche Bag Handbook, and had gotten up to five or six. So he was starting to get amorous, which Annie didn't necessarily mind. JP was attractive, as the JP's of the world usually are, and the thought crossed her mind that she might go home with him. She knew he was a lout, but there was something attractive about his loutishness, which is part of the reason why guys like me hate him so.

So JP is getting worked up, and he wants to tell our lady a little story about his sexual prowess, or the time he squandered the nest egg of an unfortunate senior citizen or something, so he leans in. But it being a nice restaurant, there are candles in his way, so he pushes them to her end of the table. JP then takes her hands and pulls her in closer. He talks for a moment or two when suddenly…smoke starts to rise. He pauses, a distinctive smell rising up from the table, and poor Annie notices something's wrong. Her head feels hot, in a not-good way. She looks down at the candle and realizes…"Holy Shit, my hair is on fire!"

She explained, and I can attest, that she wears a fair amount of product in her hair, so that shit really went up. We're talking flames here, and everyone in the restaurant freaked out. Well everyone except JP, who of course was used to pressure situations, usually involving losing other people's money, so he was cool as a cucumber. With Annie sitting across from him, hair ablaze, due--at the very least--in part to him, JP did nothing. Nothing! He just looked at her, a little shocked. Then, slowly, amazingly, a smile began to spread across his face. Like someone had told him they'd like to buy some high risk mortgage-backed securities, JP's grin began to grow, and soon enough he was laughing. Laughing in the face of the girl he had just set on fire. Annie tried to pat her hair out with a napkin as the I-Banker just sat there giggling away. Finally, mercifully, he started to move his arm, and she thought for sure he was reaching for a cup of water to put her out. Annie waited, thankfully, for this disaster to end. JP's arm came up into view from under the table and wait–no, that was not a glass of water in his hand, or a napkin, or even a little note that says, "Sorry I'm such a douche bag." Nope, instead it was a cellphone. And JP lifted it up and took a picture of his date who was on fire. Let me say that again...he took a picture of his date who was on fire. Because really, how can you not a capture a moment like that for eternity? He took two photos then sat back and smiled at his incredible good fortune.

Finally a waiter ran over and smothered Annie's hair, putting out the fire. She was relieved, and JP was a little disappointed. At that point in telling me the story, Annie pointed out the part of her hair that was still a bit damaged, but honestly, my mind was already racing. Clearly there was work here that needed to be done. My Internet date, who had blessed me with a story containing the sentence "The thing about deaf kids is that they can't hear you, like, at all," actually had a far crazier story of her own. Sure, finding your job annoying is one thing, but getting your hair lit on fire?! That's comedy gold! I mean, awful, but comedy gold! That's when I knew it was time to start writing this stuff down. Because only in Internet dating do your bad dates have their own far worse bad dating stories. The whole enterprise is like a long line of hilariously sad dominoes. You topple one disaster, and it just leads you to another tragedy waiting to fall. And we've all had to endure it. There is no online dater out there who says, "You know, actually, all my dates have been pretty super!" We're all pissed. We go on dates hoping to find the best, then have to figure out what to do when we get handed the absolute worst. And we still have to buy the worst a couple of free drinks. So that night, I started a website: It'sNotAMatch.com. And that site ultimately led to this book. In the following pages you'll read some of my horror stories, as well as the lessons I've learned along the way. I can't promise it'll make you a better Internet dater, but it will make you a happier one. Because hopefully you'll laugh, and know that the next time you're sitting across the table from a terrible date, you'll have plenty of company when you say "I'm sorry, but we're really just not a match." And then smile, because hey, at least your hair's not on fire. Probably.

So here we go. On with the disasters. But first, a little bit of advice...

CHAPTER 1.

CRAFTING THE PERFECT EMAIL

When I joined Match.com many years ago, it was for one girl: Shadoe987. Sweet, sweet Shadoe987. So lovely, so innocent, so eccentric in her spelling choices. I had taken a half-hearted swing at Match a few years prior, so they had me on their "bother to the point of insanity" email list. They sent a plea with a silly headline like "Look at All You're Missing Out On!", then a simple little picture of Shadoe987 and a few sentences about her and, well, it got me hook, line, and also sinker. "Yes, look at what I am missing out on!", I said to my cat as I happily entered my credit card number. There was just something about Shadoe987, she was so...attractive, so wholesome, so forgiving. The kind of girl who would absolutely not judge you for being duped by yet another promotional email from a company you had no interest in. So I signed up for Match, fired off a carefully crafted message to Shadoe and a few other incomparable young women, and waited for the responses to come rolling in. And you know what happened? Jack shit.

I never heard back from Shadoe987. Who knows where she is now...maybe living in Paris with her ravishing yet reliable husband who's taught her more about wine than she ever imagined possible. Or maybe she died in a horrible farming accident. One of the two. But I will always remember her fondly for the lesson she taught me: Internet dating is a numbers game. It's the first thing I learned about Match, and so I think it's right that it be the first thing I share with you. Because after I didn't hear back from Shadoe987, I emailed 15 or so other women with a far less carefully crafted message and you know what? Five of them wrote back. Five! That's a lot of people. Sure, 10 totally ignored me, and the subsequent dates resulting from those five responses were awful BUT...I got five dates. In a half-hour of work. And suddenly my mission was born: create a formula for the perfect introductory email and send it to as many women as possible.

Look, if you wanna send every person you meet online a delightfully personal email that took you 20 minutes to craft out of thin air, go for it. You're a gentleman and a scholar. But you're also an idiot. I'll say it again: Internet dating is a numbers game. And they're not small numbers, they're really really big ones. It is more likely that the person you're writing WILL NOT write you back, no matter how charming and eloquent you are. Believe me, Shadoe987 got every bit of my charm and eloquence and she didn't even thank me before she died under that tractor. So, in order to be an effective Internet dater, your first email should be something quick, chipper, and seemingly personal. Then you can move on and be seemingly personal with the next guy. Your note can be an average, forgettable two-line message, OR it can be the most genuine and well-intentioned form letter in the history of the written word. I recommend the latter.

Listen to what I'm going to tell you now: the recipient CANNOT know that you are sending them a form letter. If they do, you're done for. I've seen some mass emails that men have sent, thinking they're carefully disguised, and it's enough to make you weep. Long paragraph that's just about them? Form letter. Vague platitudes about how "pretty and cool" the lady seems? Form letter. Random jokes about how crazy the world of Internet dating is? Form letter. And last but not least: epic, rambling love poem in broken English that gets uncomfortably sexual in the final stanza? Sadly, that's also a form letter. How do you avoid making your email look like a form letter? By not making it a form letter at all.

A form letter is repeated word for word to each recipient. What I have instead is an equation, and it is perhaps my greatest Internet dating secret. The perfect introductory email has taken me years of trial and error to develop, and got so good that at one point my response rate was up to 50%. That's right: 1 in 2, motherfuckers. My intro email is my best friend, and I know every step of it by heart. If I ever get sent to some awful prison in a Midnight Express-type situation, my introductory email is what I will recite in my head to keep myself sane. Some men put their children on their knee and tell them about the time they scored the winning touchdown in the big homecoming game–I will tell my son about the time I created the perfect email that let me meet fantastic women. OK, a few fantastics and a lot of crazies. Now I pass the formula to you. Guard it with your life.

PART 1: A LITTLE ABOUT THEM

This is where the magic happens. Read your future betrothed's profile, find one thing that strikes you as funny or interesting, then write two sentences. One sentence is too brief to make a good impression; three sentences is desperate hand-wringing; two sentences is just right. This is real, this is genuine, this must be original for each person you write. See, not a form letter!

PART 2: A LITTLE ABOUT YOU

OK. I lied. It's kind of a form letter. Part 2 can be the same every time. But your goal in this section is simple: in as funny a way as possible, tell them a little about yourself, accentuating your most dateable characteristics. If you're tall, work it in casually. If you do something heart warming and awe-inducing like teaching deaf kids (but not just for the money), subtly drop that hammer. And if you've got a great rack, just say the word BOOBS. Guys will figure it out.

Now, if you'd like to write this section out longhand every time to feel better about yourself, feel free. But I copy and paste, because it's always the same, and because my schedule is packed with tons of important business meetings. (Note: I consider watching Gilmore Girls to be an important business meeting.)

PART 3: SAY GOODBYE

That's it. Say goodbye and sign your name. Plain and simple.

Seems so obvious, but it's not. You'd be amazed at how many first emails are a complete disaster. People write "Hey, what's up, baby?!" then hit send. Or, even worse, they write six paragraphs, say they know they're going on too long, go on even longer, then apologize apologize awkwardly and probably start crying. The perfect intro message is basic: highlight what you like about them, what you think they'll like about you, and get the fuck out.

Is it dirty pool to use a prewritten formula on someone I'd genuinely like to date? Yes, and I don't feel great about it. But as I said, Internet dating is a numbers game. All I'm really doing is increasing the odds of finding the perfect match. But I'll warn you, these powers must be used for good. Should you turn evil and use this formula just to get laid, then I will find you and I will kill you. I mean, I won't, because those Gilmore Girls appointments are really piling up, but seriously, don't. It's uncouth. Use the perfect email formula only to find the person that's right for you, and both I and the Gods of Love and Internet will smile down upon you.

Unless that girl happens to be named Shadoe987. In which case, she's totally not writing you back. (May she rest in peace.)

CHAPTER 2.

THE GIRL I TOOK TO A CONCERT

I have a long held rule about taking dates to the theater. I love theater. And I love girls who love theater. But I found that every time I'd ask a girl to check out the next big thing on Broadway, she would happily accept, allow me to shell out big time for the tickets, then break up with me as soon as humanly possible. It's happened at least five times. It got to the point where they had to change the stage manager's announcement to, "Please silence your cellphones, refrain from taking flash photography, and abstain from breaking up until after the show has completed. The crying is becoming a distraction." After a few years of this nonsense, I made a new rule: never take a date to the theater. If I were smart, I would've banned concerts as well. But if I were smart, this book wouldn't exist. So let's all thank God for small miracles...

In my one and only attempt at Internet speed dating, I met one girl who said she was afraid of mirrors, another who admitted that she'd never dated a man who hadn't read *Lord of the Rings* and wasn't gonna start now, and Janis. Internet speed dating is similar to regular speed dating, except that a website shows you the other daters in advance, so you can read their profile and learn a bit about them. So it basically lets you have several Internet encounters in one evening–which is great, because in the time it normally takes to have one bad date, you can have fifteen little ones that are just as bad. But Janis was surprisingly, alarmingly, cool. She had The Big Three: good looks, intelligence, and sense of humor––which would be awesome were it not for the 11 other men there discovering that at the exact same time. I urged her to dumb it down for the rest of the guys that night, maybe rub a little mud on her face, perhaps conjure up a decent fart every now and again. She laughed, accepted my phone number, and promised she'd call. A solid fart joke can do that to a woman.

As we all know, the surest sign that a woman isn't going to call is that she promises she will. But miraculously, a few days later, Janis rang me up and invited me to her apartment. A solid fart joke can do that to a woman. I arrived, and it was clear that there was some serious chemistry going on. There was laughter, there was banter, there was an unprecedented level of charm. It was like that bedroom scene from *Out of Sight*, if someone swapped out George Clooney with a 30-year-old version of Brian Dennehy. OK, a 30-year-old version of Brian Dennehy who had a stunning disdain for the guidelines of modern fashion. But I was witty that night, friends, and I was winning the lovely Janis over.

She was a big music fan, so we talked about our favorite albums. Or, she talked about her favorite albums, and I talked about the albums I pretended to like more than the soundtrack to Cocktail. We looked through her iTunes and I suggested some bands she might like, even though I really was just repeating names I'd heard my cooler friends talk about at parties. ("The Mountain Goats can't possibly be the name of a group, can it? Oh, it is? Then yes, I love The Mountain Goats.") Popular music isn't my specialty, but I managed to discuss it for 15 minutes without looking like a complete jackass, which was fortunate, because that's about how long it took for Janis to say this...

Janis: It's funny, I know we only met a week ago, but I feel like I've known you for so much longer than that.

Me: I know, you're right. (Smiling, leaning in for the kiss...)

Janis: (Holding up her hands, stepping away...) Which is why I think we're going to be really, really good friends.

Boom goes the dynamite! It's amazing the moments women choose to announce their desire for friendship. At the mall, washing your car, riding a rollercoaster. Whenever, really. I'm confident that when I die, my wife will pick up the jar of my ashes, carry them tragically to the front of the church, and whisper quietly to the lid, "I think we should just be friends." And the women in the church will nod to her and mutter supportively, "good call."

So, Janis felt we should just be friends. Which made sense, because we did meet at Speed Friendship, not Speed Dating. Honestly, it wasn't crushing, I didn't know her very well, but it certainly was a surprise. The night was going well, dammit! If talking convincingly about music didn't move me above friend, what would? Janice asked me if she had hurt my feelings. I told her "No," and I apologized for misreading the signs. Janis said that was alright, and then did the only logical thing she could in that moment: grab me, pull me close, and start viciously making out with my face. Boom, again, goes the dynamite.

Janis: I'm sorry, I just really wanted to do that.

Me: Uh…

Janis: Do you want to go to a concert some time?

Remember those *Choose Your Own Adventure* books from when we were growing up, where at several points in the story you got to choose which direction the hero went? Well now it's time for us to play a little *Choose Your Own Adventure*, tragic dating-style…

If you would like to A) Say "Yes" to Janis and attend a concert with her, assuming that she's realized what a fine match you are, and hope there's romance on the horizon then…keep reading.

If you would like to B) Politely decline and get the hell out of there because clearly this girl is nuts then…go suck an egg, because that's not what I did and I'm not writing a whole fake ending just because you're boring and can't make fun choices.

I said "Yes" to the concert, kissed Janice again, and went on about my evening. Awesome, right? RIGHT?!

Here's the thing about the concert. It wasn't just one of those show up a 7, have a few drinks, see some music then roll out of there at 11:30 kinda concerts. It was a FESTIVAL. That's right, a motherfucking festival. In New Jersey. I do not now, nor have I ever, lived in New Jersey. And because it was a festival, that meant it lasted all day. And because it lasted all day, that meant it cost $150. What did I do when presented with this horribly unappealing information? You're not gonna make me go through that whole Choose Your Own Adventure silliness again, are you? I bought a ticket and packed a lunch.

Playing at the concert were: Radiohead, Girl Talk, and A Bunch of Motherfuckers No One Has Ever Heard Of. And, as is the law at outdoor summer music festivals, there were three different stages, so even if you were lucky enough to know and like one of the bands who's playing, you'd be constantly annoyed by the sound of the other two bleeding over from across the field. It was like eating a sandwich filled with something you really love, like turkey, and then having a guy walk over every few minutes and stuff something random in your mouth along with it, like chocolate-covered gummi bears. Or dirt. Or really bad bongo music. In a word, it fucking sucked.

But that wasn't the worst thing. The worst thing was that after Janis and I arrived, at about 10 AM, it started to rain. I forgot to bring an umbrella, so I had to buy a $50 hooded concert sweatshirt, which might as well have had "I'm a Sucker" written on the back of it in big black letters. What it actually had written on the back was "Death Cab," which as it happens, means pretty much the same thing. Oh no, wait. You know what? That wasn't actually the worst part. The worst part was when, about 10 minutes later, as Janis and I searched for a dry patch of grass on which to spend the next seven hours, she said, "So, you know we're just friends, right? Anyway, I think I'm gonna try being a lesbian for a while." That was definitely the worst part. And... look at that! We're officially out of dynamite.

Yeah, Janis, it turns out, wasn't just uninterested in me, she was uninterested in my entire gender. And she chose to tell me this not before I bought the concert tickets, nor before boarding the ferry for a 45-minute commute to another state, but before the 20 minute mark of a seven-hour day together in the rain. A solid fart joke, you see, can do that to a woman.

I, for one, really wish I had chosen a different adventure.

CHAPTER 3.

EVERY INTERNET DATING PROFILE EVER

There's really only one rule to follow when creating your dating profile: Be Different. OK...wait, there's two rules. Be Different, and Avoid Hardcore Racial Slurs. Alright, fine. Three rules. Just three. Be Different, Avoid Hardcore Racial Slurs, and Abstain From Using The Phrase "Sweet Ass Titties." Other than that, you can do whatever you want.

Seriously though, standing out is all that really matters. Let's say Match has a million profiles online. At least nine hundred thousand of 'em are going to say the same boring crap over and over again. "Long walks on the beach," "someone who really listens," blah blah blah. If you wanna get read, all you have to do is be one of the remaining hundred thousand who says something interesting. I don't care how you do it, but Be

Different. Even if it's a little nuts. Here's a profile that recently caught my eye...

> *"Secretive conservative sensory quiet mastered the art of listening without the words."*

That's it. That's the whole thing! Maybe she's crazy, or really *super* foreign, or just operating on a different plane than you and I (one, apparently, without sentence structure)–but either way, I remembered her. No way in hell I'm sending her an email, but two weeks later she's still occupying some space in my mind. Not the prime real estate admittedly, but it's space! That's all you're looking for. Jump out to your reader, wake them up, make them forget all the ridiculously lame profiles they just read and stop at yours. What's the best way to do it? Avoid every lame-ass Internet dating cliche in the book. If you've seen someone else–or more likely, thousands of someone elses–write it, come up with something better. In fact, let me make it simple for you. In case you're new to the online romance game, this is a summation of Every Dating Profile Ever Written. Avoid these sentences at all cost.

(First, start with a photograph taken from so far away that it's impossible to tell if you're cute, or even human. Then hit 'em with the prose...)

ABOUT ME

Gosh, what do I say in these things? [**Anything really, just try to avoid cliches.**] LOL! [**Oops. Too late.**] I NEVER dreamed I'd be signing up for Match, but I know a bunch of people who've had good luck on here, so I figured, why not give it a shot? [**So...your heart's not even really in this? Good to know.**] Hey, if we hit it off, we can just tell our friends we met in a bar! [**Exclamation point! For no reason!**]

OK, sorry, I got off track there. [**You were never really on track.**] I'm just not great at talking about myself. [**Oh, I have a hard time believing that.**] But...if you asked my friends and family, they'd probably say I'm loyal, hard working, but still totally laid back. [**Your friends and family think you're a St. Bernard?**] I love to laugh and have a good time [**Everyone does. That's why it's called a "good time."**], and I'm just as comfortable in a cocktail dress as I am in a pair of blue jeans. [**What a relief. One time I dated a girl who was uncomfortable in blue jeans. Can you say, "disaster??!!!??"**]

I love to travel, either to the beach, or somewhere exotic and off the beaten path. [**Again, we all do. They're called "vacations."**] On the weekends you can usually find me either dancing the night away in a club downtown [**To find you there, I would have to go there first. Which is probably not happening.**], or on my couch watching a DVD. [**Wearing either...a cocktail dress OR blue jeans!**]

WHAT I'M LOOKING FOR

I am looking for someone who knows what he wants. [**I want to click on the next profile.**] Someone who likes to work hard and play hard as well. [**In–God knows–how many different kinds of dresses or pants!**] Sense of humor is a must for me! [**I can see that.**] I need someone who can make me laugh, whether it's after a hard day of work or people watching after brunch. LOL! [**It seems to me you'll laugh at anything. You just laughed out loud at a sentence that you yourself wrote and doesn't have any jokes.**]

I want someone I love spending time with [**a daring stance**], but who understands that sometimes I need a night with just my girls, and he can hang with the boys. [**Are there people who can't do this?**] Oh, and I know it's cheesy…[**Never stopped you before**], but he MUST love dogs. [**Can I love dogs, but not like you? Is that an option?**] Above all else, I need a man who's honest [**the last guy cheated, didn't he?**], and can always cheer me up when I'm having a bad day. [**"LOL?" No "LOL?" I thought that one had LOL written all over it.**]

Sorry, I'm totally rambling now. [**Don't be too hard on yourself. You've been rambling since the beginning.**] If you've gotten this far, you should totally send me a message! I don't bite, I promise! LOL! [**I knew it. LOL.**]

What do you think? Are you ready to be my partner in crime? [**Well, I'm considering a crime right now, but the role I had you in mind for was not "partner."**]

And scene.

If you think I'm being too harsh, you're probably right. But trust me, everyone reading your profile is thinking the exact same thing. So if you really want to meet someone, be original, be creative, and try as hard as you can to be funny. Pull even one of those off, and I promise you'll be remembered.

LOL.

CHAPTER 4.

THE GIRL WHO DRANK TOO MUCH

Dating without drinking alcohol is a little like working out in your dress shoes. You can do it, but you're gonna look like an asshole. I believe strongly that every first date should last exactly two drinks–one is too brief, and three is too tipsy–but I see nothing wrong with getting entirely *Leaving Las Vegas* for every date following. Look, dating is hard, and Internet dating is damn near impossible, so there's no shame in relaxing yourself with a glass of wine or, say, a gin and tonic IV. Especially if you're gonna be expected to have sex. I mean, have you seen people have sex? It's gruesome. You can't reasonably be asked to sleep with someone for the first time without getting a little loose first. But there's a fine line between drinking to become relaxed and drinking to become a total nightmare. This story is about the latter.

Over the years, I've had a fair amount of experience with boozehounds. In college, my freshman-year roommate used to throw up on the floor next to his bed so often that after a month or two he stopped trying to clean the carpet and just cut the dirty pieces out and threw them in the trash. He also listened to Dave Matthews Band incessantly. He and I were not close. Later, I had a friend who liked to get drunk and pee in my cat's litter box. Let me tell you, you haven't lived until you've tried to clean a human amount of pee out of cat-sized pee container. Kinda like being a nurse in the ER, except without all the glamour and disposable gloves. But a girl who I met on Match a few years back seemed nothing like these characters. Betty was adorable, intelligent, and a doctor. Doctors are all well adjusted and totally stable, right? RIGHT?!

Far from a party animal, Betty was actually a little shy at the beginning of things. She was working on her dissertation, and our dates often finished early so Betty could go write. In fact, several of our nights ended with little more than a polite kiss and her darting off to the subway. And honestly, I was totally fine with that. Why rush things, you know? I like to be really sure about a girl before I get intimate with her, just to make sure she can, you know, handle the disappointment. So things with Betty were going at just the right speed, for a while.

After about six weeks, it was plain to both of us that we were ready to move forward. We had plans for Saturday night, and Betty made it clear that she would be spending the night. I'd like to think I didn't do a fist pump, but let's be honest, I probably did a fist pump. I bought some wine, got my roommate out of the apartment, and waited for her to arrive. 8 o'clock...nothing. 9 o'clock...also nothing. 10 o'clock...nothing still, and then my phone rang. I picked up, and heard someone who sounded a lot like a girl I knew, if she had been on spring break for the last, say...three and a half years.

Betty: Helllllloooooo?

Me: Hey. Where are you?

Betty: Helllllllllooooooooooooooooooo?

Me: Yeah, hi? Betty, are you there?

Betty: I don't...uh...I don't think my phoooone is worrrking.

Click. Dial tone.

I don't know about you guys, but when I'm getting ready for a night with a lady friend, I like to shower, shave, put on a nice shirt and then...get totally fucking shitfaced. To the point where I no longer know how to use a telephone. She called again...

Betty: Helllooooo?!

Me: Yep, still me.

Betty: Oh, Hi. Hi, Hi, Hi. I don't think my phone is working.

Me: So I've heard.

Betty: Sorry I'm late. I'm out with my sister and she won't let me leave! Isn't that mean?!

Me: Well, maybe this isn't the best night for us to get together. It sounds like you've had quite a night.

Betty: No, I'm fine. I'm totally...I just. I didn't eat dinner. I'm totally, totally fi–

Aaaaaaand then she hung up again. There were four more calls, each less intelligible than the last, and all ending in an inexplicable hang up. I wasn't angry, just a bit annoyed, and suggested we reschedule for another night. If you're gonna wait a while to sleep with someone, you might as well add on another week just so it doesn't feel like something out of a National Lampoon movie. The only problem was, Betty was just getting warmed up.

I don't know whether she had been hiding the drinking up until then, or if she just got a real taste for the sauce after the Night of a Thousand

Phone Calls, but I'm not sure I ever experienced a truly sober Betty again. She was probably nervous about our relationship and the pressure that waiting a while had put on things, but hey, so was I. At least I had the decency to mix in a few low level hallucinogens with my alcohol to keep from being a total bore. Eventually we did sleep together, but I think we both felt like the spark was gone. The vague scent of Jaegermeister can do that to a relationship. Finally I decided to meet Betty for coffee and call things off.

Here's a tip, friends. When you're picking a place to break up with a girl because of how much she drinks, do it in a location where she's won't be able to drink. Otherwise, the following is going to happen.

Me: So, um, I think we should talk.

Betty: Yikes. This sounds serious. OK, I just need to go to the bathroom first...

And that's when she stood up, stumbled, and knocked over our entire cafe table. Glasses were broken, wine was spilled, and two innocent salt and pepper shakers lost their lives for no reason at all. It was like something out of a Courtney Love documentary. There was a crash, people looked, I was embarrassed. Betty, however, was totally cool, and pranced happily to the bathroom, unaware of the destruction she'd left in her wake. We had been at the bar for, MAXIMUM, forty-five minutes.

How she'd gotten so drunk in that time, I have no idea. But when she returned, all she wanted to know was why I had knocked over the table and, more importantly, what had happened to her cocktail.

I told her I'd walk her home, and on the way explained that I thought we should stop seeing each other. She seemed fine with it, although I can't be entirely certain she actually heard me, because halfway through the conversation she yelled, "Fine! Whatever! Just buy me one more drink," and pulled me into a neighborhood dive bar. Because that's what the evening was missing: one more drink.

When we walked in, the bartender nodded hello to me, then looked over at Betty. Immediately, his face fell. He looked...well, he looked like the Japanese do when they see Godzilla coming. There was terror in his eyes, ladies and gentlemen, and it was clear to me that he had met young Betty before. She sauntered up to order, and I could tell the bartender was wrestling with his fight or flight instinct. His actions said "Sure, I'll give you two drinks" but his body language cried "Just don't break anything this time." Betty mumbled something and returned with two beers. I reminded her that I'm allergic to anything made from wheat, so she smiled, took a sip from each beer, and happily sat down. And within five minutes, the head of the girl I had just broken up with was somehow asleep in my lap. I looked at the bartender and we shared an understanding shrug. I had a feeling both of us had been there before.

I finally got Betty home, on the elevator, and, after several disapproving looks from the neighbors, through her front door. She stumbled through her apartment, I helped her into bed, and I said goodbye for the last time. She lifted her head from her shoulder, muttered "I'm sorry," then passed out on her pillow. Me too, Betty. Me too.

CHAPTER 5.

OKCUPID: WHERE NO QUESTION IS TOO PERSONAL

"Which pubic hair style do you prefer for a partner?"

1. Natural
2. Neatly Trimmed
3. Completely Shaven
4. It Doesn't Matter.

This is one of the quandaries that OkCupid poses in their questionnaire section. Something the site feels it must know to correctly match you with your partner. Do you like pubes neat or completely shaven? (Come on. Natural? Are we neanderthals?) And then, once you've made that high impact decision, you get to choose how important that answer is to your quest for a mate: Irrelevant, a little important, somewhat important, very important, or MANDATORY. As in, "It is mandatory that my partner's crotch be neatly trimmed, otherwise I really don't see the point in going on living." OkCupid is a strange place.

Truth be told, pubic hair is one of the tamer topics in OkCupid's "Questions" section. I made this discovery when, after tiring of my results on Match, I decided to try another site. The first thing they do when you sign up for OkC is ask for your profile, then run you through these Questions. Sure there are the basics, like, "Could you date a smoker?" or "Do spelling mistakes annoy you?" but then things get pretty dark, pretty fast. There are sections on ethics, religion, and culture, but those often get brushed past on the way to the sex questions, probably because that category seems to have been crafted by a serial killer. And the most shocking thing is that these responses MATTER. If you read the fine print, OkCupid readily admits that your answers to these questions are the sole determining factor in who they recommend to you as compatible. Agree on matters pube and otherwise, your "Match Score" will be through the roof. Disagree, and the website will be less likely to show you to each other. Yippee! The questions are written by users, but OkCupid vets them and decides which ones to ask you, specifically. To get a sense of how insane this is, here's a sampling of some of those questions. And yes, they are all totally real.

Would you ever consider cutting a partner (who asked for it) in sexual play?

First of all, no. And second of all, WHAT?! Is that a thing? Are people out there cutting each other during sex? To serve what purpose? Because they always felt the one thing sex was missing was a ton of blood? I can't remember the last time I was making out with a girl and thought "Man, I really wish somebody would stab me right now." Sex is complicated enough, we don't need to be introducing knives into the equation. For the record, I answered "Maybe" on this one, just in case Freddy Krueger has a hot sister.

If a partner asked you to have sex in a sex shop booth with others watching, would you?

I'm not even entirely sure what a sex shop booth is. Where people watch porn inside the sex shop, because watching it in the privacy of their own home has become common and predictable? That sounds awful. And why would these people ever want to watch me have sex, when they can admire the work of skilled professionals on the little sex booth TV screen in front of them?

If a clone was made of you, would you sleep with it?

Really? Something that's not even scientifically

possible? That's required to find me a girlfriend, Cupid? Is this a personality questionnaire or a Stanley Kubrick movie? And no, sir, I would not have sex with my clone, because I know how I get afterwards–the weeping, the non-stop text messages, it's just not worth the trouble.

How does the idea of being slapped hard in the face during sex make you feel?
Terrified? Is terrified an option?

Have you ever gone on a rampant sex spree while depressed?
Ok, that's literally something they ask serial killers. What's next, "Did you ever kill small animals as a child?" Let's say, for the sake of argument, I have gone on a rampant sex spree while depressed. (Spoiler alert: I haven't. When I'm depressed I eat pieces of chocolate that have been filled with peanut butter.) What possible reason is there for me to share this with a prospective lover? On the chance that she, too, is a rampant sex spreer, and is looking for someone of a similar spirit? No one would ever be looking for that. That's deranged. Basically this question boils down to: "If you click 'Yes,' you will immediately become undesirable to everyone on the face of the earth. Would you still like to click 'Yes'?" Because I am a savvy Internet dater, I clicked "no." And ate

another Reese's.

How would you feel about a partner self-stimulating while you are performing oral sex?
Why, are we making a porno? How complicated is this going to get? Should I buy a swing?

How many people have you kissed that are not related to you, in a more than friendly way?
Well, that seems like a reasonable--wait, why did you say "that are not related to you." Why is that necessary? Why would I even think that you're asking how many people I've had romantic kisses with including THE ONES THAT I'M RELATED TO? That number's definitely gonna be zero, right? We're not romantically kissing people we're related to, riiiiight?

Would you consider roleplaying out a rape fantasy with a partner who asked you to?
Depends. Are we talking about one of those light, playful, fun rapes?

Do you think you can determine how good someone is at sex based on how they move on the dance floor?
Oh God, I hope not. Please don't let this be true. PLEASE.

If your partner wanted to pay for you, as a couple, to see a professional dominatrix, would you go?

As long as she's a professional. I have had it up to here with amateur dominatrixes! And I'm glad we got the finances out of the way early, because my biggest problem with going to see a dominatrix as a couple is who would foot the bill.

After reading these questions, I began to think none of them were meant for me. That my sex life was hopelessly mundane and out of touch. Then, finally, I found a nice, normal query that made me feel right at home. We'll call it the cherry on the top of the Crazy OkCupid Sex Questions Sundae...

While in the middle of the best lovemaking of your life, if your lover asked you to squeal like a dolphin, would you?

YES! Obviously yes! I have, and will again. In fact, when I think sexual satisfaction, I think, "What would Flipper do?" My lover need not even request it. So thank you, OkCupid, for having at least one question I can identify with!

As you might have guessed, I returned to Match pretty soon thereafter.

CHAPTER 6.

THE SEX CRIER

At this point in the book, you're probably getting the impression that Internet dating is just one disastrously awkward first date after another. But that's not true. Sometimes there's a disastrously awkward second, or third date as well. And, if you're really lucky, on rare occasion, you may achieve a full-fledged disastrously awkward long-term relationship! But that's only if you really apply yourself. Thankfully, on one or two occasions, I have been so determined...

I met the Sex Crier on a rare two-date evening. It's something I try to avoid, but if scheduling becomes difficult or I'm particularly eager to meet someone and feel like I can't wait another day (I know, I'm unimaginably romantic), I'll plan two dates on the same night. It's not a great idea, but if you manage your liquor carefully, it can be done. Just avoid telling the same stories or jokes to both of your dates, because no matter how big a cad you are, somewhere deep inside your soul will just up and break. But Sex Crier was the second date on a two-date evening, and within minutes she had blown the first one entirely out of my memory.

I still remember what she was wearing and even what she smelled like, in as unserial-killer a way as possible. I had to talk her into the date, as she was reluctant to date a cat person (she has allergies), or a writer, and I am guilty of both. (Although my cat won't consider me a writer until I land a three-picture deal.) Sex Crier was a lawyer, you see, and had found that she usually matched best with other lawyers. Boy was she wrong. Me not being a lawyer had nothing to do with us not getting along. It was more the constant 100% insanity that did it.

On our first date she made me laugh immediately, which usually means I'm hooked. And she was outstanding to look at, which never hurts, but there was something a little…off about SC. Her stories were a little crazier than they should've been, her frankness a little franker than it should've been, and she just had a strange energy going on. You know when you meet someone and sense right away that they're not like other people, but you can't figure out whether that's a good or a bad thing? That was her. She was what 75-year-olds call a "firecracker", and warned me in no uncertain terms that I should stay as far away from her as possible. "I'm crazy," she said, after I walked her home from our first date. Already feeling swept off my feet, I replied "I don't think you're crazy at all." I meant it as a compliment. Unfortunately, I think she took it as a personal challenge.

We dated for a few months, and I think we broke up eight times. Which is a lot, considering I don't believe we ever explicitly said we were an item. She just liked breaking up, and was constantly honing her craft. She worked tirelessly at it, forever trying new techniques and approaches. She was the Michael Jordan of ending things, the Bill Gates of deciding we'd be better off as friends. Wanna break up in a crowded restaurant at the top of your lungs with tears and profanity so everyone stares at you? She's got a move for that. Or maybe split up via text message for a reason she won't explain and very possibly does not herself even know? Please, Sex Crier can do that in her sleep. (She even did that once. Maybe she was just dreaming, but I distinctly remember being awoken by the mumbled words, "it's not you, it's me.") Or, and this was my personal favorite, wanna break up after a homeless man asks me for spare change and I say "sorry, man" in a way she deemed "not caring enough"? Sex Crier owns the copyright on that shit. That's her Sistine Chapel, and let me tell you, seeing it in person...it'll take your breath away.

Anyway, she liked drama. And because that made our relationship fairly volatile, I thought it best to hold off on having sex for a while. I still tend to attach, you know, personal feelings to the making of the whoopee, so--since she was breaking up with me on a weekly basis--I felt the need to self-protect. Why did I keep dating her at all? No idea. She was smart, funny, and pretty. The Big Three! What am I supposed to do to fight that? She was kryptonite to my Superman. Sure, it was insane kryptonite, and I look ridiculous in a cape, but I was powerless against her. Ultimately, finally, I agreed to cash in her one-way ticket to Sexy Town. And yes, that's what I called it. You can see why she found me difficult to resist...

So, we're in bed and we're doing the stuff and after a bit we start triumphantly, heroically, having sex. The way Zeus did it, I'm sure. Then, almost instantly, and without any notice, she starts crying. Deep, baleful sobs, like her dog had just died. She wasn't in pain, and it wasn't because the sex was just so gosh-darned good either, believe you me. Even the women in my fantasies are only barely tolerant of my lovemaking technique--so it wasn't that she had finally realized how good sex could actually be. She was upset. About something she refused to discuss. The next ten minutes or so played out like this...

Me: Is something wrong?

SC: Yyyyyesss.

Me: Can we talk about it?

SC: No.

Me: Please, I'd really like to talk about––

SC: Just keep fucking me!

….Aaaaaaaand repeat. I'm telling you, you haven't felt true sexual satisfaction until you've done it under duress while being drenched in a shower of your partner's tears. For the older gentlemen out there, if you ever run out of Viagra, just encourage your lady to start desperately weeping while forcing her body upon you. It's a proven aphrodisiac.

Every few minutes, Sex Crier would be so overcome and need to take some time to really focus on the crying. I would try to be supportive and ask her if she wanted to talk about it, while quietly celebrating what was hopefully the end of the evening's awful intercourse. And look, I didn't blame her for the tears. Clearly there are many serious and totally justifiable reasons to find sex upsetting. Especially if you're having it with me. I just didn't understand why we had to keep having sex through all the upset. I would ask what was wrong, she would ignore my question, cry a bit more, and then initiate more tragicsex. It was like getting raped by Judy Garland.

Finally, mercifully, after maybe 20 minutes, my body decided that it was done having sex for the evening. In my head, I was high-fiving my manhood for coming up lame, but Sex Crier was upset. Which makes sense because clearly she was having such a good time. She flopped down on the bed next to me and sighed with disappointment. "That's it?" she said. "Yup," I replied. "But I haven't finished," she declared. I decided to go with silence as my response to that one. "So you're just…done?" she asked angrily. "In more ways than you know," I thought to myself, but didn't say out-loud because I'm a wuss. Instead I went with "I'm sorry, but if we can't talk about what's wrong, then I think we should just go to sleep." And that, apparently, was the last straw. I guess after inexplicably crying on a guy for a half-hour, she was used to being dutifully brought to climax. Great deal if you can get it, but I was not offering such an arrangement. So she rolled over, looked me straight in the eyes, and said "I can't believe you!" Then she got out of bed and disappeared into the other room.

When I like a woman, I give her a lot of leeway. Too much, sometimes. I don't know why. It's just that being with a great girl makes me really happy, and if she's got some quirks and rough spots, well, I'm open to working that out. We're all imperfect, and hell, I've got more rough spots than sandpaper––I mean, I said "Sexy Town" back there--so I try to be flexible. But tonight would be the end of my flexibility with Sex Crier. I walked into her living room after a while and found her angrily reading a book (which I didn't even know was possible). She looked up, said "I don't want to talk to you, I'm too upset" and returned to her novel. That was when I decided to show her a break-up move that even she had never attempted.

The "Have Sex While Being Cried On For a While, Get Yelled at For Not Delivering Orgasms Under Those Conditions, Then Initiate a Break-Up With a Girl You're Not Even Officially Dating While She Pretends to Keep Reading Her Book" break-up was patented that fine day, friends, and it was a beauty. There was crying, obviously, and a lot of yelling, then several phone calls afterward where she told me that I was a son of a bitch. It lacked evidence as an assertion, but she was a lawyer so I had no hopes of winning that argument. And frankly, I was in no mood to quibble. I had been with The Sex Crier and was happy knowing that our ninth breakup would be the one that stuck.

CHAPTER 7.

THE GREATEST FIRST DATE CONVERSATION STARTER EVER

The waitress drops off your drinks and you stare after her longingly. Look at how free she is, walking around, talking to whomever she wants, laughing at all the fun-loving things that happen in a day, not a care in the world. But not you. You're stuck sitting across from the Conversation Monster. Every topic you raise, she chews up and spits out, then waits for you to try again. It's awful. Your "A" material is long gone, hell, you blew through your "D", "E" and "F" stuff before the menus even came. Now you're considering talking about the weather, if only you could remember what the weather was like before you entered this vortex of boring. Was it raining, or were those just your tears? Your date looks at you, wanting to kill herself, and you look back, begging her to take you with her. The evening is not going well.

But then...you think of something. Something you read in a weird book once. A promise of a topic so fertile, so rich with conversational opportunities that it can save any date. But the author of the book seemed like kind of a wacko. I mean, he was always going out on such terrible dates, could you really trust his advice? What sort of a person does that? Plus, you bet a lot of those stories weren't even true. But what have you got to lose? This topic can't be any worse than the twenty other ones your date batted away since you sat down, right? RIGHT!

So you go for it. You lean in, and immediately your date can tell you've got something. There's a twinkle in your eye, a little spark that says, "I'm about to knock your motherfucking socks off." She leans in to meet you, then you open your mouth and say...

"Would you have sex with a dead person for five seconds if it meant getting free laundry for the rest of your life?"

And then you sit back and watch while her mind explodes.

I know what you're thinking. "That's the single greatest conversation starter ever?! It's disgusting. And weird. And you're weird." Well, all of that is true, but trust me, great bonds have been formed over the epic Dead vs. Laundry Debate. I've seen many a slow happy hour, a weary cocktail party, or an otherwise respectable wake set on fire by

Dead vs. Laundry. I've used it to talk to people who hated me, didn't know me, or didn't care to, and every single one of them came out a friend. Except for the people at the wake. They were a little creeped out.

Here are the terms: you must have sex with a dead person for a full five seconds, but no one will know. The person is recently dead and can be whatever gender and physical appearance you wish. You walk into a room, do the grossest thing ever for five seconds, and then you leave. No one's the wiser. And in return, you get the laundry. Oh sweet, sweet laundry. No, this is not drop-off service. This is not pay-by-pound, clothes-come-back-dirtier-than-they-went-in laundry bullshit. This is magical. It's like the Harry Potter of laundry. Any item you drop in your hamper appears immediately cleaned, pressed, and folded, waiting for you in your closet. We're talking sweaters, suits, dresses––whatever you want to be cleaned. Hell, throw some silverware in there and see what happens! It's magic, for God's sake. And it continues FOR THE REST OF YOUR LIFE.

OK, obviously having sex with a dead person is unpleasant. We can all agree on that. But free, immediate laundry for the rest of your life?! I mean, come on! Look at this. You see what's happening here? I'm getting caught up in the debate! I'm sitting here by myself and debating with my computer as I type. That's how gripping the issue is. But that's not what I'm here to do. I've already made up my mind. (Answer: Fuck yeah, dead person. Let's get it on. And just like that, this book has been banned in 29 states. Yippee!) I'm here to urge you to try it out. Bring up Dead vs. Laundry on your next crummy Internet date, and watch the romance unfold. How?

First of all, it's a provocative question. Your date will immediately feel more personal, more intimate, just because you had the balls to bring it up. And it's controversial, so you and your date will almost certainly have passionate feelings about it. Passionate agreement: great! You two see eye-to-eye on even the most trying of topics. You were made for each other! Passionate disagreement: also great! You're the David and Maddie of Internet dates, sparks are flying, will they or won't they, what's gonna happen next?! Of course, there is the third option. Passionate certainty that you're a total freak. But who'd want to go out with a fuddy duddy who thinks like that, right? RIGHT!

So next time you're in a conversational quagmire, go for the gold. At the very least, you'll learn a lot about the person you're with. If she goes for the deal, then you know she's a risk taker, a controversial thinker, and, perhaps, horrible around the house. If she turns down the deed, then you've learned she's more straight-laced, thoroughly sane, and very possibly never going to call you again. But she'll remember the date. She may go out with a cooler, taller, better looking guy next week, but she'll never forget the man who asked her if she'd do a corpse for laundry. And, just like when you're building your profile, being remembered is what it's all about. I'll take that over two boring drinks any day.

CHAPTER 8.

THE GIRL WHO WAS A MENNONITE

Do you know what a Mennonite is? Neither did I. Mennonites, it turns out, are a traditional, peace-oriented religious group that can be like casual everyday Protestants, or, if they think life's just too easy, can be a lot more strict. Like...ride your horse to work strict. They're not Amish, or Quakers, or Candlestick Makers–thought are often confused with them because some Mennonites (the super popular and fun to hang out with ones) refuse technology and dress in the funny clothes with floppy hats. As religions go, hardcore Mennonites are not terribly progressive, and their views on premarital sex, divorce, alcohol–in fact, pretty much everything we laymen call "fun"–are, again, pretty fucking strict. So strict that if they read half of the words in the last sentence, they would probably pass out. So strict that a lingering stare counts as getting to second base. In short, Mennonites are not the sort of folks that any normal person would ever think to date. But lucky for you, dear reader, I am not normal.

The sentence, "they have all these old, lugubrious looking tires" is what sold me on her. I know, sexy, right? Well, during my first drink with Marcia the Mennonite, we got to talking about Costco–because I know how to sweet talk a lady–and she had recently bought tires there. "Were they a good bargain?" I asked. "I don't know," she said, and then explained how flat and lugubrious they were. You know, your standard flirty romcom conversation. Except the thing was, I didn't know what lugubrious meant. I'd heard it before, probably used it wrong a few times, but to know exactly what Marcia said, I had to go home and look the word up. And for me, that's as romcom as life gets. A girl who uses a word that I don't know is a girl who immediately jumps to the top of my list. Which probably explains my past relationships with "Tumultuous Tina," "Horticulture Hannah," and "Triskaidekaphobia Diane." But Marcia was funny as well, and entirely adorable. So it didn't really bother me when she told me she grew up Mennonite, and lived that way for the first 25 years of her life. Now, when she added that a few years earlier she had a long-term relationship with a man she agreed not to kiss until they got engaged, that did give me pause.

And not a short pause, either. A pause long enough for me to check my watch and make sure it wasn't still 1927. But what can I say? I'm a sucker for vocab. She said she wasn't very religious anymore, and was drinking enough beer to back that up, so I decided to go for it. Before date one had finished, I'd already asked her out for date number two.

Obviously, before our next meeting, there was research to be done. After looking up lugubrious (It means sad and mournful. Who knew?!), I googled Mennonite aggressively. The Internet revealed a range of Mennonite activity: everything from women churning their own butter to girls wearing bikinis on the beach. (And no, there were no pictures of Mennonite ladies churning butter on the beach, you pervert.) But which ones were the real Mennonites? The ones who looked like background players from *Witness*, or the girls on a very wholesome spring break? I didn't know. I was intrigued enough by Marcia to try to find out, but I realized I was going to have to ask her some awkward questions. There was no other way to know if the potential of us dating was a worthy pursuit. Here was my list of concerns.

1. Would I have to go to church?
2. Would we get to have sex?

That was pretty much it. And really, isn't that what it's always about for men? If we date, how frequently will I have to be bored and/or annoyed? And in return for this annoyance, how often will we get to do the sexies? If the ratio is promising, dudes can usually make it work. However, in the case of Marcia the Mennonite, this trade-off was totally up in the air. I mean, have you seen *Witness*? I know they were Amish, but that was best intelligence I had, and it didn't exactly play like a chapter of "Penthouse Letters." So, going into date number two, I had a lot of questions to ask.

Marcia must have sensed something was on my mind, probably because of her Mennonite superpowers, because after a few drinks, she generously turned the conversation toward her love life. And thank God--strict horseriding God or otherwise--she did, because I had no idea how I was going to do it. Asking someone from a religious background how often they take a trip to Funky Town is no easy feat. But Marcia opened the door, so all I had to do was walk through it.

Marcia: Honestly, this is all pretty new to me. I don't think I've ever had what you would consider a normal relationship.

Me: What do you mean? What makes it abnormal?

Marcia: Well, the physical part...

Me: (trying to play it cool): Oh, do you not...? Have you never...?

Marcia: I've never had sex.

And even though record players no longer exist, and her grandparents probably thought they were the devil, a record scratch could be heard in the distance. I was on a date with a very nearly 40-year-old virgin. A 36-year-old virgin, to be exact. And honestly, it didn't bother me in the slightest. In fact, I thought it was sweet. Marcia went on to say that she was no longer waiting for marriage, that she didn't believe in that anymore, but was planning on having her first time be in the course of a serious, long-term relationship. She asked if I was looking for a long-term relationship, and I told her truthfully that I was. And then we smiled and continued on with what proved to be an outstanding second date. She didn't say lugubrious again, but hey, you can't have it all.

Did I find out whether I was expected to go to church? I did not, but don't get greedy. I accomplished one of my two missions, and was happy with the answer I found. Should I have been more wary of someone so inexperienced? I don't know. I don't really see why. I'm not exactly Wilt Chamberlain myself. And I liked her, so I didn't care about anything else. If anything, I felt a little bad for Marcia. I mean, if all went well, I would be totally ruining the first sexual experience of her life in a few months, and you've got to feel for a woman who has to face that. But the upshot was she didn't have anything to compare me to, so maybe she wouldn't really mind. Or at least not realize how much she should've minded. And all that had me feeling pretty good. Pret-ty, pret-ty, pret-ty good. (Because I'm selfish.)

Now, despite all this openness and good feeling, making the first move still wasn't any easier. Two dates down, and I still had not given Marcia my patented (somewhat disappointing) first goodnight kiss. She said she wanted to take things super slow, understandably, and I wanted to respect that. As date number three was winding down, however, I started to feel a little anxious. My usual plan with first kisses is to take all the pressure out of it, to make it feel like the inevitable culmination of a fun and flirty night. Put a hand on the knee while talking, or rest my arm on the small of her back while walking around. Nothing creepy, no yelling "put the lotion in the basket!" or anything, just some subtle physical signals. But Marcia was not playing along with my plan. My palm was on her knee for about two seconds before she darted off to the bathroom. I tried some playful hand holding, which went about as well as invading Russia in the wintertime, and it was pretty clear I was getting nowhere near the small of her back. She guarded that thing like it was the family jewels. And come to think of it, based on her sexual experience, maybe she thought the small of her back was the family jewels. I don't know. But I was thrown, so I just kept telling myself "Mennonite, Mennonite, Mennonite." She wasn't used to this sort of thing, so I just had to stay confident and on course. It would all work out in the end.

As I walked Marcia to her car, I knew it was now or never. I'm all for taking things slow, but three dates without a smooch sounds to me like a wonderful way to start a friendship. We were walking down an alley which was a little high on the dumpster-to-darkness ratio for a first kiss (you're looking for no dumpsters and a lot of darkness, FYI), but I decided to go for it. I stopped, turned to her, then smiled and leaned in, when…

Marcia: I'm seeing someone else.

Again, the devil record scratch. WHAT?!

Marcia: I'm…seeing someone else.

You're seeing someone else? But you're…a Mennonite! The last guy you dated you wouldn't kiss until…marriage…and you wouldn't let touch your back…and you've never had sex…and…you're a Mennonite. WHAT?!?!?!

Of course, I didn't say any of these things. I think I said "Huh?", and Marcia tried to explain. She had met someone at the same time she'd met me, and she had already started "making out" with him, and didn't feel comfortable "making out" with two people at the same time. Which under other circumstances would be totally understandable, but wasn't exactly the message I was expecting from a girl who had been a virgin longer than I had been alive. I mean, when you discover a lady's ancestors found zippers too socially progressive, you don't really expect her to be playing the field.

Me: Well, we're still in the early stages here. There's no need for us to be exclusive.

Marcia: Oh, I couldn't do that. It just wouldn't feel right.

No. Of course not. THAT wouldn't feel right. Dating two guys while you act like Anne of Green Gables is totally cool, but kissing them both in the same week would be too much to handle.

Marcia: But I do like you. Would you be interested in maybe dating, but not kissing or...doing anything at all...sexual?

And thus she tried to pitch me on essentially the exact same relationship she'd had with her previous beau, the man who wouldn't get to kiss her until they wed. Which, incidentally, is the exact same relationship I have with my sister. And all my female friends. Which is why I'm trying to date on the fucking Internet! Anyway, it was quite a twist from Marcia the Mennonite, one that M. Night Shyamalan would've been proud of if his movies were still any good. And it left me dumbfounded. I thought I was being an open-minded good-hearted guy, trying to go at a slower pace, while actually I was just wasting time while another dude swooped in and stole my conservative Christian. As I walked back to my car, alone, I shook my head and muttered to myself. I'd never felt so lugubrious in all my life.

CHAPTER 9.

WOMEN VS. SHORT GUYS: INTERNET DATING'S FIERCEST GROUND BATTLE

Short Guy #1: The problem is that women don't want to date me because I'm too short.

Short Guy #2: I know, me too!

Short Guy #1: I mean, it's not even like I'm that short.

Short Guy #2: Yeah, no, me either. I'm not that short either!

Short Guy #1: I wish there was some way to get to know a girl in a setting where she didn't realize how short we were. Talk a bit, share some interests, fascinate them with our minds, but only later do we reveal our tiny legs.

Short Guy #2: Yeah! Only later!

Short Guy #1: And it's not like I'm even that short.

Short Guy #2: No, I don't think you are.

Short Guy #1: You either! I mean, we can totally reach things that are on high shelves.

Short Guy #2: Or we can get a ladder.

Short Guy #1: Or we can get a ladder. Absolutely.
  (Pause)

Short Guy #1: And we'll have pictures!

Short Guy #2: Pictures?

Short Guy #1: Women will assume we're short, because they can't see us. And when they can't see us, women always assume it's because we're hiding how short we are.

Short Guy #2: They do. They do always assume.

Short Guy #1: So we'll put pictures up that make us look regular-sized–or even tall! We'll use tricky angles, or clever point-of-view techniques, or just show them only our faces! It'll be impossible to figure out our actual height.

Short Guy #2: Yes! Clever point-of-view techniques!
  (Pause)

Short Guy #2: They'll ask.

Short Guy #1: Hmm?

Short Guy #2: They'll ask how tall we are. They always we do. Sometimes even when they're looking right at us they ask. Just to make us say it out loud and confirm their suspicions. I hate it when they ask.

Short Guy #1: Hmm.

Short Guy #2: Or over time, they'll make us list it. They'll make us list our height upfront, with our other interests and general descriptions. We're done for. Sure, we could leave it blank, but they'd see through that in a second!

Short Guy #1: Hmm.
　(Pause)

Short Guy #1: I got it!
　(Pause. Short Guy #2 looks at Short Guy #1 expectantly.)

Short Guy #1: We'll lie!

(Short Guy #1 and Short Guy #2 hug triumphantly.)

And thus Internet dating was born.
　Men have numerous gripes about Internet dating: Women don't write back, or they post out-of-date pictures, or they're not as impressed by

one's ability to stalk them as they reasonably should be. But women have only one complaint: Short guys lie. That's it. That's the only thing that bothers them. Believe me, I get all the emails.

As I mentioned earlier, this book began as a website. And within weeks of it going live, without me even requesting it, women began writing to complain about short dudes. I'd say for every 10 emails I got from female readers, at least six were decrying the lies perpetrated by the under 5'6" community. (The remaining four out of 10 emails were restraining orders. I'm choosing to believe they were SPAM.) Here's one of the many notes I received...

> "What if you just constantly met short guys online? What does that mean? That's one huge reason why I stopped online dating. They were all short and lied about it. It's like, hey, eventually, I'm going to find out you're fucking 5'6? and not 5'8?. And maybe that makes me shallow, but we all have our dealbreakers. Can't do short. Also can't do pointy shoes. No and no."

Aside from the alarming negativity towards creative footwear choices, this comment is fairly indicative of the messages I got. As is its ferocity. "I'm going to find out you're fucking 5'6? and not 5'8?." I mean, that's a curse word. Over two measly inches! It sounds like the sort of thing that would be written in cut-out magazine letters, and come wrapped around a severed finger. "You lie about your height, I cut off your hand!" I don't think I'd even notice that someone who claimed to be 5'8? was actually a ghastly 5'6?, but it sounds like these women would happily stab such a person in the gut. Presuming they could reach that low. And trust me, she's not alone. So...what's the deal?

I'll admit that I don't know a ton about this issue, because I'm 6'2." (That's right, ladies! If you ignore the fact that I write books about all my dates, I'm a real catch!). I've asked around, and the most common explanation I get for female height preference is that they like to feel "surrounded." They want to hug someone bigger than them, lie next to someone large, someone who can put their arms around them and really...surround. So then I had to ask around and find out what the fuck that meant.

The best I could come up with is that tall men make women feel, for lack of a better term, protected. Comforted, cozy, and looked out for. Height, apparently, subconsciously offers that. It better be subconscious, because I'm tall and I'll tell you right now, I ain't protecting you from shit. If a murderer, or a burglar, or even a strong wind should enter your room in the middle of the night, me and my 74 inches are getting the hell out of there. At least a short guy can fit under the bed, so there's a decent chance you'll have someone to hide with. I'd keep that in mind.

Sadly, though, out of this innocent preference, a war has been born. Women like tall dudes. Short guys, viewing this as another in a long series of slights (see: genetics, also: overhead compartments), grow frustrated and turn to Internet dating. Women, finding men lacking in general (can't fault 'em on that one), gradually migrate to Internet dating as well—only to find it largely populated with the same short fellows they disregarded earlier. Shortstacks, now tired of their continued and seemingly arbitrary dismissal by women, get pissed, say "fuck it", and just start lying about their height. Now the women also get pissed, and before you know it, the only people not angry on Match.com are guys like me. And truth be told, my natural disposition is kinda grumpy, so now we're all fucked. All because of a desire to be "surrounded."

So what do we do? When I discussed height on my website, I got greater responses—both in volume and vitriol—than I had ever before. People started fights, called each other names, and several men confessed to me that the trouble with their height had sunk them into a deep depression. So I think it's time a treaty was signed. (Yes, men, we will provide step ladders so you can reach the table.) Women, you can be more accepting of guys who are a little shorter than you'd like, and maybe take a chance on somebody who is awesome but doesn't fit your narrow-minded vertical requirements. And Napoleans, you can do your best not to lie or mislead about your height, even though it is often held unfairly against you. If we can all do that, then, perhaps over time, the war between women and short guys will subside. Perhaps.

But if not, allow me to remind you, ladies: I'm 6'2"!

CHAPTER 10.

THE GIRL WHO DID HEROIN

There are two ways you can handle a date after you realize you're not a match. You can shut it down, giving this person you will never see again as little energy and effort as humanly possible, or you can have some fun. You can say, "I've got to be up early tomorrow," or you can say something you've never said on a date and see what happens. Like, "I'm throwing out my nail clippers and going with bite-only trimming from now on." Or, instead of asking for the check, order a Clamato Bloody Mary and see how it flies. Rather than asking about her family, ask about the last person she wanted to murder. I've done all of these things, and, admittedly, each one was a complete disaster, but at least I got something interesting out of the evening. I'll take that over two forgettable drinks any day. Who knows, if you pledge to do the unexpected, you might just find out you're sitting across from a heroin user–and isn't that what Internet dating is all about?

The moment I arrived to meet Courtney, I knew something was up. She lived in a neighborhood I'd never been to, so I let her pick the bar–something my chivalry (or, at least, my desire to fake chivalry) would never normally permit. When I got to the bar, it was dark. Like porn theater dark. I understand the value of ambiance, but the mood was less "romantic rendezvous" and more "hide my horrific cold sores." It was an odd location to meet someone you were hoping to recognize from a two-inch picture, but I tried to keep an open mind. I sat down under the brightest lightbulb I could find and waited for Courtney to arrive.

A few minutes later, the door opened, and while I couldn't see the lady's face, I did get a glimpse of something. Something…long…and silky…and white. Was she? Could she be wearing…? Yes. She was wearing opera gloves. And it was definitely my date. We weren't going to the ballet later. We weren't at some hipster cocktail spot where the bartenders wear visors and name drinks after dead abolitionists. Hell, we weren't even in Manhattan. But for some reason, Courtney was wearing a sequined top, knee-high black boots, and a long pair of white opera gloves. It's the sort of thing Catwoman would wear on a date. Which is fine if you think I'm gonna propose, or I'm Batman, but we were in a dingy little dive bar in

Crown Heights, Brooklyn, that *she* had selected. They didn't have napkins, but she had silky white gloves. The last hour of *Inception* made more sense than this. All of a sudden, I was beginning to crave some clam-flavored tomato juice.

We talked for a while, and it was clear that Courtney and I were not a match. Through the darkness I could see that my attraction to her wasn't strong, and clearly we had different tastes. She liked going all out: fancy parties, trendy clubs, shirts that looked liked disco balls. Meanwhile, my idea of a perfect evening includes an expertly TiVo'd episode of *The Good Wife* and a sandwich that achieves just the right ratio of peanut butter to jelly. She was more Paris Hilton, while I was more Staying-in-a-Room-at-the-Hilton-Hotel. Eating-Toblerones-from-the-mini-bar. Clearly there would be no second date, but that didn't mean I couldn't make our first one as interesting as possible.

Me: So, what do you do for a good time?

Courtney: Oh, you know, go to parties, have drinks with friends, smoke some pot here and there, the usual...

Me: Sure, but what do you do for a *really* good time?

Now, that is not a question you should ask on a first date. It's not appropriate, too invasive, and let's be honest, a little creepy. But because I was never going to see her again, I really had nothing to lose. Plus, she wore opera gloves on a random Tuesday night. What are the chances that the hardest thing she'd ever done was a little marijuana?

Courtney looked at me in a way that made clear, even through the Edgar Allan Poe lighting, that she had information to share. I tried to put on my best "you can trust me" face, which looks a lot like my "you can't trust me" face, but with less winking and twirling of my imaginary mustache. She thought things over, then decided to go for it. Yippee!

Courtney: What are the hardest drugs you've ever done?

Me: Well, I've tried pretty much everything, but I usually stick with the light stuff. (Wildly untrue. I've tried pretty much nothing, and don't really know what "the light stuff" means, except maybe light beer, which I'm horribly allergic to. But you can't say "beer upsets my tummy" to a girl you're trying to out as a druggy, so I did the best I could.)

Courtney: Cool. Well, I've tried pretty much everything, too. But I just found the best heroin delivery service, if you want me to give you the number.

DING DING DING! We have a winner! Lame date results in knowledge of heroin delivery service, simply by asking one slightly inappropriate question! Did I want the phone number? Hell no. I wouldn't even know how to begin using heroin. Does it work as a mixer? Can it go with iced tea or diet root beer? Because that's all I've got in the house. If I tried dialing a heroin delivery service, my telephone would laugh and send me a text that said, "Who are you kidding? You can't inject heroin, you're afraid of Q-tips." (My phone's a real jerk.) But that didn't stop me from urging Courtney to continue...

Apparently, you text a guy named "Steve." Anticlimactic, I know. I was hoping for "Coltrane," or maybe "Heroin Pete." An hour or so later, Steve shows up at your house with a box of different kinds of heroin, and you select your favorite. The options, I believe, are: "Kate Moss", "Kurt Cobain", or "The Brother from Diff'rent Strokes." You give the guy $100, and just like that, you have yourself a nice little sack of heroin! It's like ordering a pizza, but with less carbs. Steve leaves, you do some heroin, and moments later you're thinking up bad ideas for Nicholas Cage movies. It's just that simple.

Needless to say, you should not under any circumstances tell your date you know a great heroin delivery service. I admire Courtney's honesty and trust, but if I hadn't already taken myself out of the running long ago, I sure as shit would have done so the moment she uttered the phrase "favorite kind of heroin." But, after learning about this odd little part of society, I was able to honestly consider the night a success. We finished up our drinks, and when I told Courtney I had a great time that night, I truly meant it. I'm not sure she felt the same, but luckily she had some Black Tar back at her place to make it all feel better.

A mismatched date doesn't have to mean a bad one, as long as you've got the balls to make a good one happen. And you may not have to drink a single drop of Clamato to make it happen.

CHAPTER 11.

CAN YOU EMAIL SOMEONE TWICE?

Honestly, I think the woman of my dreams probably doesn't email people back right away. Certainly not the ones she meets online. First of all, she's busy. She has a demanding career in the field of writing for SNL/teaching literature/ impersonating Connie Britton/being the first female manager of the Boston Red Sox. On top of that, she has her hobbies. The girl of my dreams just doesn't feel right if she can't spend at least an hour a day writing jokes/playing guitar/cleaning up oil spills/training to be the first female manager of the Boston Red Sox. So I understand if she doesn't respond to my first email quickly, she probably gets so many. It'll take her a day or two to wade through the other losers and come upon the majesty of my message. She will open it and immediately see that I am The One. She'll recognize my humor, my intelligence, and my obvious demonstration of an almost supernatural sexual appeal. But what if, even then, after she's saved the rainforests and adopted all the stray puppies and called for the perfect suicide squeeze, what if the girl of my dreams still doesn't write me back? What do I do then?

Simple. I write her again.

Hold on. What?! You can't write someone twice! You're harassing them. You're becoming one of those deranged Internet daters who copy and paste every message, who live in a different state, who have only the loosest command of the English language, who never ever ever take "no" for an answer. That's what people say to me when they ask if they can email someone twice. Then, calmly, sagaciously, in a manner that no doubt reflects the wisdom of the Dalai Lama himself, I respond, "What's the worst thing that could happen? She's gonna not write you back...again?"

Look, is emailing someone twice before they respond a good idea? Generally, no, it is not. It's a little weird, and unless handled with the utmost grace, could put you in that most dreaded of dating categories: Desperate. In fact, I'm not sure there's a more dreaded dating category than Desperate. Pedophile, maybe. That can be a tough sell. Or Enthusiastic Fan of The Band Creed. Nobody likes that. Taxidermist Who Stores His Work in His Private Home, that's also problematic. But desperate is bad, and if the ladies get one whiff of it, they're out of there. Which is why a double email situation has to be handled with extreme care. But really, what have you got to lose? She already hasn't written you back, the situation isn't gonna get any worse. So buck up, be a man/woman, and take a chance. But to make that chance a perfect chance, here's what I suggest...

Hey, Man/Woman of My Dreams, [except don't actually say "Woman of My Dreams." That's the kinda shit that gets the Feds involved. Believe me.]

OK, I know this is a dangerous move, sending a second email. It veers alarmingly close to "behavior of an Internet crazy", which believe me, I am totally aware of. But you seemed really great in your profile, and I couldn't resist taking another shot. Someone who [cite something specific from their profile that you like that isn't her boobs, you superficial prick], is someone I just gotta know.

So anyway, I hope to hear back from you. I promise I'm only 50% as crazy as this seems.

[emoticon of your choice, if you're that sort of person]

Aaaaaaand BOOM. There it is. The perfect second email. It has worked for me, I don't mind telling you, more than once. And by "worked," I mean led to an awkward and ultimately disappointing date with someone who in retrospect was very obviously not the woman of my dreams. But that doesn't mean *you* shouldn't try. Go for it! Your chances are immediately improved by your sheer lack of being me.

Now, let's say you're unconvinced. It's understandable, I'm kind of a lunatic. So don't take my word for it, listen to Olivia. Olivia is a woman who caused quite a stir on my website recently when she wrote in and described the Match experience from an attractive lady's point of view. Annoyingly attractive, really. I've seen her profile, and believe me, she is both lovely and quite smart. The total package if you will. (Annoying, right? I'm annoyed. But she is also very nice. Which is such a typical total package thing to be.) Here is what Olivia said about second emails...

> I honestly don't mind when someone emails me twice. In fact, I probably respond to more second emails than first emails. I get, on average, 50 emails a day. **(It's OK. I yelled "Oh, give me a break!" too.)** When someone starts off by saying they're emailing me again, it's like I feel bad for ignoring them and thus I pay more attention to them. And only about 10% of guys send me second attempt emails.

See that! You can make an attractive person feel guilty by sending a follow-up email! Isn't that worth the effort all on its own? And you're setting yourself apart from the crowd. It's a win-win. Look, worst case scenario, there's someone out there who knows you tried extra hard to get in touch with them. How bad is that? In fact, I think it's a little sweet. And if they think you're a douche for it, well then screw them. Right?! RIGHT!

Unless you like Creed, in which case, they're right, you are a total douche.

CHAPTER 12.

THE GIRL WHO MADE ME DANCE

There are a few people out there who actually know how to dance. They have a sense of rhythm, are naturally graceful, and have spent enough time dancing that they can acquit themselves without looking like they're having a seizure. Then there's the rest of us. We look like we're having seizures. And we're in the majority–by, like, a lot. In America, there are 300 million seizure dancers, and then maybe...23 people who know what they're doing. (Right now, to yourself, you're thinking that you're one of the 23. But you're not. Trust me. Your friends know you're not, they just don't want to tell you.) But I have always felt that all you really need to do to *seem* like you know how to dance is to simply appear like you don't give a shit. Of course you give a shit–because we all give a shit–but looking like you don't care if you're dancing well is often as good as dancing well itself. I'm not talking about being in a music video or dancing with the Rockettes or anything, I'm just talking about going to party and moving around in a manner that doesn't prompt people to ask whether you've forgotten to take your medication. It's a matter of confidence and joy, that's all. But even knowing that, even though I possess the secrets of dance and the code to passing as a happening human being, I am still, when on a dance floor, the biggest doofus on the face of the earth. And the woman who forced me to prove that to her, well, she has never forgiven herself, I assure you.

It started out improbably well. Paula was attractive, far more attractive than I had any right to obtain, and with each date she just got better looking. The first night, she looked great: dressed to the nines, beautifully made up, topped off by a gorgeous figure, and things only improved. The next time we met, her outfit was even more striking, and Holy Moses, a good bit more revealing. On the third date she looked hotter still, and by our fourth encounter it was starting to get uncomfortable. I mean, the discrepancy in our appearance was getting absurd. It was like I had gotten into one of those Make a Wish arrangements without being a child or having a terminal disease. She looked *that* good. And she was cool, too. Smart, cute, with a great sense of humor: The Big Three, as you've heard me say. Also, she spoke a few different languages and had an impressive job. But there was one problem: she wanted me to dance.

She danced a lot, apparently. Two or three nights a week, she would go out with her lady friends and try a new spot. And she wasn't just doing regular dancing, she was doing shit with names. Merengue. Swing. The Mambo. Skitterbug. Is Skitterbug a thing? I'm pretty sure I made that one up. The point is, she was such a good dancer that she had a variety of moves that other people had heard of. I have one move. It's called "Trying Not To Look Like An Asshole", and I'm terrible at it. Paula was most decidedly one of the gifted 23, and I knew that once she had figured out that I was not, we'd have a real problem on our hands. Which is why I made it my mission never to reveal my secret.

You can't really blame her. I mean, if you love dancing, and you're dating a guy who you like, it stands to reason that you'd love to go dancing with him. Of course Paula didn't expect me to actually be good; women have learned not to ask such things of us. But she did hope, at the very least, that I'd be fun. If I were relaxed enough about it to be a good time, then I'm sure Paula would've been fine with the horrible execution. She, of course, had no idea who she was messing with. I'm not relaxed. I'm not even really fun. So we developed our own little routine. Paula would ask me if I'd like to go dancing, and I would claim to be busy/tired/entering the witness protection program, and promise that I'd join her the next time. The next time would arrive, I'd agree to go, then at the last minute cancel with heartfelt regret and dismay. Once I even invited her dancing on a night I knew she was already busy, just to sell the ruse even further. It was pathetic, to be sure, but I was trying to keep a good thing going.

After a month or so of this, Paula had had enough. She didn't come right out and say it, but it was clear that if we were going to be taking things to the next level, I was going to have to meet her friends and go dancing. It was their thing, and any guy she was serious with was going to be a part of it. (The next level, by the way, is the one where you get to have sex. God, I love that level.) Really, I had no choice. Friday night, myself and four attractive ladies would be going dancing. Somebody call the cops.

I have few moves on the dance floor, and as luck would have it, each one is a catastrophe. I do a thing that's sorta like the robot, except that move requires too much skill, so I do sort of a shy robot who's afraid to cause much of a scene. His name is "Milton." I also have a step I named after my friend's mother, because I learned it by watching her at bar mitzvahs and family gatherings. You think I just made that up as a funny little joke thing, but sadly there is no funny little joke thing here. The Mrs. Knoll is a very real phenomenon.

Just ask her. Then, finally, I do something that looks a lot like running in place, because it actually is just running in place. They're all bad, and they're all the absolute best I am capable of. My only hope was that if I used them in frequent enough rotation, Paula wouldn't be able to identify any one step as especially atrocious. I just kept telling myself, "Change things up, and look like you don't give a shit. She'll never know!" It wasn't a good plan. But it was a plan.

For a while, things were going well. Paula looked amazing, of course, and had that twinkle in her eye that said "you've got a shot tonight, as long as you don't fuck this up." And, at first, I impressed even myself. Milton was oiled and lubricated, and Mrs. Knoll hadn't looked so spry in years. The group of us were dancing, laughing, and at no point did anyone ask me when I developed epilepsy. I wasn't having fun, but I think, for a brief moment there, it looked like I didn't have a care in the world. It was majestic. But then, all of a sudden, it wasn't. I looked at Paula, realized how well it was going, and started to care. I understood I had a chance with this beautiful woman and got uncomfortable. I doubted myself, I doubted the dance, and I could tell from the look on her face that it was beginning to show. And that's when I did the worst thing you can ever do on a dance floor. Yes, friends. I did…the fist pump.

It's sort of my break-glass-in-case-of-emergency move, the fist pump, except it doesn't make the emergency any better. There's not a fire extinguisher behind the glass, or a direct line to the cops, just lighter fluid, crumpled newspaper, and more fire. Personally, I find it hilarious, to stand on a dance floor and not move at all, other than an ironic, over-enthusiastic pumping of my fist. Sadly, nobody else agrees. Or, at least, not after more than five minutes. The fist pump fits vaguely in the category of rhythmic movement, so I can get away with it for a while, but that while is shockingly brief. With Paula's beautiful eyes fixed on me, I pumped my fist for a bit. Then, after she laughed, I pumped my fist some more. From that point on, I was locked in. I knew I had to stop, do anything else, even a couple of jumping jacks, but I couldn't! Her friends were looking at me and people had started to stare, but I had become too self-conscious. I knew a lot was riding on this night, and that thought alone had made any actual dancing impossible. So there, in the presence of a beautiful woman who just wanted to get down, I pumped my fist for an entire half-hour.

Needless to say, I was not ushered into the ranks of the elite 23 that night, nor into the lovely Paula's bed. She made a good show of it, pretending to be pleasantly surprised by my dancing prowess, but clearly her heart wasn't in it. She wasn't judging me or putting me down, she just knew I wasn't into something she loved, and because of that, we weren't going to work out. And she was right. I dropped the ball on this one, big time. If I could've just relaxed and been normal, I would've had a shot at an amazing girlfriend. So you see, it's not always the women in my stories who are the walking (or dancing) disasters, sometimes it's me. A disaster who can't stop pumping his fist.

It's too bad, because for a second there, I really was pretty good.

CHAPTER 13.

HOW TO BREAK UP WITH AN INTERNET DATE

Breaking up with someone you meet conventionally is pretty easy. I mean, it's not, it's the worst thing in the world, but at least you know how to do it. You meet them in person, apologize for having to do this, then brace yourself for the angry crying, or the disappointed crying, or perhaps a potpourri. How you tell someone you met online that you don't want to see them anymore is a touch more complicated.

Luckily, I am just the man to handle this delicate life event. If anyone has ended, or had end, more short-term, not-really-relationships than me, I'd like to meet 'em. Mostly so we can hold each other and cry, but still. In my experience, if you don't want to rip someone's clothes off after the second date, you might as well call it quits. By that point, you know a fair amount about the person, your chemistry has had a chance to develop, and you've probably been kinda drunk in each other's presence. If that's not gonna get clothes ripped off, I don't know what will. Other than *Hulkamania*, of course. Also, if you end things after two dates, you're in no danger of leading someone on. Though honestly, I don't really know what "leading somebody on" means. It's a phrase guys say when they're pissed off because they got dumped, but can't just scream "I'm pissed off, I got dumped!", so they made up the clever little catchphrase "you led me on!"

Now, let's say you decide that it's Not a Match (buy your t-shirt today!) with you and your Internet pal. How do you handle it? It all depends on what stage your relationship is at.

After One Date: You go out once and you just weren't feeling it. Whether it was with a lovely person or a hideous monster who stole your car, your obligation remains the same. You have to do...absolutely nothing. (Except, perhaps, go car shopping. I recommend the 2012 Toyota Corolla.) They call and ask you out: no need to respond. They send a sweet, inviting text: simply hit delete. You met them online, you've known them for an hour, you owe them nothing. If you're not interested, you are fully within your rights to say nothing and move on with your life. I will add, however, that I don't do this. I think if someone asks you out, it's nice of them to be interested and you should respond. You can send a text (phone calls aren't necessary), and this is what it should say:

> Hey, I had a good time meeting you, but I'm afraid I wasn't feeling a romantic connection. You seemed very cool though, and I'm sure you'll find someone great soon enough. Best of luck!

It's friendly, complimentary, and totally direct. Never fails. As I said, this sort of politeness isn't required, but you can never go wrong being nicer than the bare minimum. (Unless they stole your car, in which case, you should probably grow a pair.)

After More Than One Date, But Pre-Nudity: This is the trickiest area to handle. If you've made it past the first date, chances are one of you is at least a bit interested, and as you're the one breaking things off, chances are it isn't you. Things haven't gotten serious yet, but you've got to let somebody down, which, if you have any soul whatsoever, sucks. What do you say? Does this sound familiar?

> Hey, I had a good time ~~meeting~~ hanging out with you, but I'm afraid I wasn't feeling a romantic connection. You ~~seemed~~ are very cool though, and I'm sure you'll find someone great soon enough. ~~Best of luck!~~

The difference is, this time you say it to their voicemail. Voicemail is dignity's medium. It allows you to speak calmly and carefully, and allows them to tell you to go fuck yourself without you hearing. How are you certain to get their voicemail? There are plenty of phone apps that let you dial directly into someone's voicemail these days. If you aren't using them already, then really, I have no idea what you're doing with your life. Oh, and you can't say "best of luck" in this version because it makes you sound like a massive dick. Learned that one the hard way.

Now, you may be at a point in your not-really-relationship where this message makes no sense. If you've gone out a handful of times or done a good amount of kissy kissy, then the whole "no romantic connection" bit ain't gonna cut it. That's when you replace the part of the message with "I've met someone else and I want to see where it leads" or "I got out of something recently, and this is moving a bit too fast for me." It's your call. If these things are lies, and that makes you feel bad, remember that this isn't about you. This whole chapter isn't for you–I don't give a shit about you–it's for the person you're splitting up with. You're fine. You're probably already making googly eyes at somebody in line at the bank. It's the other person I'm worried about. Saying goodbye to them in as plausible, succinct, and friendly a way as possible is the goal here, and believe me, when I'm split up with, I much prefer hearing "there's somebody else" over "there's only you, and you blow."

After Nudity: Sorry, dudes, but if you've seen their boobs, you can't be a boob. Tough break. And ladies, if you've taken off his pants, you can't be a... scant? Nothing good rhymes with pans, really. Jerkface? You can't be a jerkface. If your Internet relationship has progressed to the point where clothes have come off, then you've got to call, speak to them live, and come up with your own script. Sorry, I can't do everything for you.

In this situation, there's only one thing you shouldn't do: meet them in person. Every time someone breaks up with me in person (which is often), I think the same thing: "I drove through rush hour traffic for this shit?" If I'm gonna be dumped, please don't commute. Let me handle this trying moment with the dignity it deserves: sitting in my underwear, speaking into the phone phone, on my couch. At least give me that.

Oh, and last thing. Don't ever say "I hope we can be friends." You've got friends. She's got friends. You didn't come online to make friends. Right? RIGHT!

CHAPTER 14.

THE GIRL WHO CONFRONTED ME ON NATIONAL TV

The problem with writing a book and website about dating disasters is that women generally don't love discovering some asshole out there has called them a disaster. And I don't blame 'em one bit. These women didn't ask to be written about, but I've disguised their identity, everything I've written is true, so I figure–fair is fair. I always knew, however, that sooner or later one of my past dates would get upset and confront me, and I just hoped that it would be somewhere private where we could talk things out rationally. You know, somewhere not like national TV. Unfortunately, we don't always get what we hope for.

A few years ago, *The Whatever Show* hired me to be their "Internet Dating Expert." I always bristle at such a title, because going out on a ton of crappy dates sounds a lot more like "Internet Dating Failure" to me, but hey, it wasn't my program.

Whatever was a national talk show on the Hallmark Network, hosted by Alexis Stewart (Martha's daughter) and Jennifer Hutt. Don't feel bad if you've never heard of it, no one has. That's why it got canceled. But Alexis and Jennifer were great to work with, which is why I can now forgive them for tricking me into quite possibly the most uncomfortable 10 minutes of my life. Am I leading up to a story? Yes. Yes, I am.

On the premiere episode of *Whatever*, I was introduced as: "A Man Who's Been On More Than 100 Internet Dates!", because I guess they thought "Internet Wackjob Who Probably Has Some Serious Issues" was a little wordy. I came on, told a few of my stories, the hosts pointed out how ridiculous my life is, I agreed, and we all had a gay old time. I returned for a few more shows and got used to my breezy 10-minute segments, after which I would head to the green room and steal all the peeled vegetables and mini chocolate bars I could fit into my pockets. However, in my last appearance on Whatever, at around minute nine, Jennifer started a new conversation.

Host: So, do you ever talk to people you went out with in the past to see how you did?

Me: No, I think my self-esteem is low enough already. (*Thinking: why are we starting a new topic after the segment has clearly ended? You're trying to keep me from stealing the chocolate bars, aren't you?*)

Host: Well, we have a special opportunity for you then! Someone who can tell you what you've been doing wrong!

Me: Huh? *(Thinking: I don't love how this is sounding. You can keep the chocolate bars, I'll just go...)*

Host: Just look right over there and you'll see... a girl you went out with!!!

Me: Holy shit. *(Thinking: Holy shit.)*

I turned around and, sure enough, standing just off camera was a girl I went out with a year previous, grinning like a maniac. Not at me, mind you, but at the cameras. This, you see, was her time to shine--and shine she would. Immediately I began scanning my memory for anything that might've gone wrong on our date. Had I been egregiously late or inconsiderate? I didn't think so. Did I try to kiss her and get shot down in humiliation? Not that I remembered. Did I my pee my pants? Possibly, but I was pretty sure I had sent all those women suitably apologetic gift baskets. In fact, the date was so mundane that I hadn't even written about it on my website. So what could it be?

Bette sauntered over to the set and the audience made that sort of *Ohhhh you're in trouble* sound that must not have existed before surprise guests on daytime talk shows were invented. We'll call her Bette, because the first thing she told me on our date was that Bette Midler was her hero. (Word of advice, ladies, men are rarely turned on by hearing that your personal deity is a brassy torch singer who stars in movies about terminal illness. Just in case you didn't know.) But here was Bette, staring at me on national TV, looking pleased as punch, if punch had all of a sudden developed one hell of an ego. From the glint in her eyes, I knew I was in for it.

Host: So, did you know that Brian here has gone out on 100 dates?

Bette: He'll probably have to go out on 100 more if they're as bad as ours was.

Aaaaaaand the audience was officially in the palm of her hand. There was hooting and also hollering. There were witches in Salem who'd gotten a more sympathetic public hearing than the one I was about to receive. But really, that's to be expected. If I was presented a man who said he'd been on 100 Internet dates, I'd assume he was a cad too. Even if his appearance suggested he was far more doofus than Don Juan. But this was a women's show, its audience filled primarily with women, so they were ready to pounce. At this point, it was clear that Bette had not come to tell me I was the wind beneath her wings. She continued...

"First of all, he took me to a bar that was in the ground floor of his apartment." The audience hissed. "What sort of a lazy jerk makes his date meet him in his own building?!" they were clearly thinking. A fair point. Except the bottom floor of my apartment is a laundromat, and no matter how often I'd begged, they wouldn't serve me alcohol. A damp drier sheet was the closest I could get. So Bette was incorrect. I pointed that out briefly, but quibbling would've made me look defensive, so I let it pass.

As the audience readied their pitchforks, Bette leveled her second charge…"Get a load of this: when he showed up, he was wearing a backpack! Who brings a backpack on a date?!" It was like someone set off a fire alarm. Women were laughing, screaming, doing the patronizing head shake at me as if I couldn't see them from ten feet away. I locked eyes, momentarily, with one of the only men in the audience in a plea for help, but he just shrugged, as if to say, "Sorry, man, you're on your own with this one." Fine, I admit, a knapsack is not the most debonair item to bring on a romantic evening. Previous girlfriends have mentioned it, and Alexis and Jennifer made it clear by their expressions that they were not impressed. Fair enough. I'll take that one on the chin. But what came next was really pushing it…

With the entire room on her side, Bette readied for the body blows. "So, obviously, I knew I was on a date with a guy who needed some work." The audience erupted in laughter, nodding knowingly at my hopeless unsophistication. A few of them, I'm pretty sure, high-fived. "And wanna hear what clinched it? What really put it over the top?! At 10pm, on the dot, he took out a pillbox and swallowed his medication!" And you know what happened then? Nothing. Bette looked around for shock and awe, but for the first time in eight minutes, the room didn't respond as planned. Medication, you see, is not that funny. It's usually related to an illness, and sickies are not the cornerstones of great comedy. Finally, I was starting to get a little sympathy. "Hey wait a second, maybe he is just a doofus!" I could feel the audience thinking. Suddenly Bette's foundation was beginning to crumble.

Host: Well, I carry boxes for vitamins and stuff…you must have just been taking vitamins, right?

Me: Uh…no, not really. I have things I take medication for…

Bette: But why did you take them during the date?!

Me: Because I need to take them at the same time everyday.

Bette: Why?! What are you even taking pills for?!

And that's when the tide started to turn. Because the way to convince an audience that you are fabulous and that the man who took you on a date is a brute is NOT to demand a complete list of his illnesses on national television. That makes you look, well, mean. I know this, because when I responded, "Really?! You want me to go through every problem I have here in front of the cameras?" one of the hosts said "Let's move on."

The mood in the studio had changed, and being a wily veteran of stage and screen, Bette Midler knew it was time to pull her trump card. "And the weirdest thing of all" she began...the hosts leaned in, the audience leaned in, hell, even I leaned in at this point..."was that he didn't have ANYTHING TO DRINK!" That was it, ladies and gentlemen. That was the fool-proof, die-hard, take-it-or-leave-it evidence of my romantic unsuitability: I did not, on that evening, drink alcohol.

It's too bad she didn't have a briefcase, because you could tell she was dying to slam it shut and declare, "Case closed!" Only problem was, now everyone pretty much hated her.

Bette had presented me as a kinda geeky guy who doesn't really know how to handle himself on a date, has medical issues, and perhaps a drinking problem. A surprisingly accurate sketch, but not one that's going to get a room full of women to yell "Get the bastard!" As it happens, I am not an alcoholic, I was just taking some time off from drinking after being diagnosed with a gluten allergy (See. I told you. Geek.) The pills were partially to aid in treating that, and to partially to help maintain the winning mood and disposition you see in these pages before you. Nothing serious at all, but I wasn't going to spell that out. The room was on my side, and I was going to let the Divine Miss M sweat it out.

Host: So, obviously, you guys didn't have a great first date, but would you like to go out again?

Me: *(pause for effect, look to audience, then...)* Are you out of your mind?

(Room erupts with laughter. Thinking: How could we have ever doubted this guy?! He's the best!)

Bette: I'm taking some time off from dating right now—no men, no women, nothing.

(Audience members roll their eyes, mutter to each other, and the battle has ended.)

Host: Alright, thanks very much, guys. Stay tuned for more *Whatever*, after the break!

(The audience applauds, Bette gets up and exits.)

Hosts (quietly): We're sorry, she seemed crazy!

Me: You're telling me. I had to go out on a date with her.

After I got off camera, the producers immediately apologizes. "We're so sorry! We thought it would be fun and playful, but she was just really mean." I assured them it was fine, which it really was, because at the end of the day, everyone pretty much told the truth and it made for some great drama. Bette, I remembered then, was a performer–a cabaret singer, of course–and was probably hoping to get herself a few minutes of TV. Or maybe she really did hate our date, and felt it unfair for me to be criticizing others when I'm no gem myself. With which, admittedly, I don't entirely disagree. Either way, the joke, however, was on Bette. The segment, it turned out, was so unpleasant that *Whatever* decided not to run it all. It would be left on the cutting room floor, and I would be left with only the memory of the time when, for about eight minutes, 200 female audience members totally hated my guts. It made it all worth it however, when several of them stopped me outside and apologized for booing me. "We're so sorry," they said, "you're better off without that one!" In fact, one of the ladies offered me her daughter's phone number. "She's adorable" she said, but added one word of warning. "Don't wear the backpack, darling. That really is uncool."

CHAPTER 15.

THE GIRL WHO BROUGHT HER BOYFRIEND

I imagine, at this point, you're asking a pretty serious question.

"Dude, why the hell are you still Internet dating?"

I get it at least once a week from my friends, twice a week from my shrink, and I'm pretty sure my cat has been building up the courage to ask for a few years now. It's a reasonable point. Why, after enough terrible dates to populate a website and write a book, and only a handful of encounters that can reasonably be deemed successes, am I still trying to meet people online? I mean, if every time you opened your front door, a guy hit you in the face with a hammer, you'd probably stop opening the front door, right? Not me. I just keep running into that hammer over and over again. I do it because, first of all, the economy's not great, and who am I to pull front-door hammer guy's job out from under him? And second, I stick with Internet dating because I've found traditional dating to be no less brutal, complex, and fraught with disappointment. Am I leading up to a story? Yes, yes I am...

Several years ago, I worked for an Internet company. Not one of the really good Internet companies that provide an important service to the world, like Google or Amazon or CakeFarts.com. No, I worked for a website that sold decorative roosters made from dried hay and twine. That wasn't our only product, of course–you can't build an entire company on poultry crafts alone. We also sold tea cozies made to look like Scooby Doo, and toilet plungers with sparkly streamers sprouting out of their pink polka-dotted handles. Because America's number one complaint about the toilet plunger has always been its lack of panache. In a general sense, we sold gifts; but only the sort of gifts you would give someone the moment before you told them you never wanted to see them again. Gifts that, when unwrapped, make you immediately regret ever having met the person who gave them to you. Gifts that even the wrapping paper feels uncomfortable being involved with. "Wait, you're not going to wrap me around that George Washington toothbrush holder, are you?" Shitty gifts were our trade, and my job was to write the copy promoting said shit. I was the one who had to convince the shopper that a highly flammable rooster made out of lawn clippings was actually the ideal thing to give their 5 year-old nephew. It was easily the worst job I've ever had, and I hated every second of it.

One day, however, a new girl arrived at the office. Until then, my co-workers at this website, let's call it ShittyGifts.com, had consisted primarily of deeply religious Filipinos and older gay men. I don't know why. I think maybe the company was started by one gay dude and a devout Filipino, and then they each just hired a bunch of their friends. But needless to say, I was not exactly knee-deep in romantic opportunities at ShittyGifts.com, or conversations-based-on-similar-interest opportunities even. And then, Tracy arrived. Tracy was two years younger than me, equipped with a quiet but wicked little sense of humor, and cute as a button. OK, fine, a busty button, if you're going to twist my arm for details. And she and I, well, we hit it off.

Quickly, Tracy and I established our own flirty little rhythm. I'd get up to get some coffee, and Tracy would walk over and ask if I had heard the new Elliott Smith album. Then we'd joke and banter and joke and banter until someone who had more power than us gave us a look that said, "Get back to work, hippies." Tracy would head to lunch, and I'd ask if she wanted help stealing extra samples from Whole Foods. The CEO would call us all in for a big meeting, and Tracy and I would compete to see who could most convincingly pretend to throw up in the garbage can. (Winner: Me. Loser: Also Me.) It started out as I'm sure most office flirtations do, with the simple discovery of someone who helps the day go by quicker. And at ShittyGifts.com, believe me, that was a hell of a discovery. But as the months progressed, it turned into something else. Something that, much to my horror, had me LOOKING FORWARD to work everyday. And when work involves crafting a complimentary description of a wall sconce made entirely from a petrified Barracuda–you know you've got something serious on your hands.

Because office romances are complex, and because, deep down, I'm a buffoon, Tracy and I lingered in the flirty-friendly-datey-paly stage for way too long. Like...two months too long. And that can be hard to come back from. I had started seeing her outside of the office, but they were never explicitly dates. They were flirty hangouts, and they never ended with a kiss. So I decided it was time to get serious. One Friday afternoon, I decided that the time had come. I would ask Tracy to go out that weekend, and at the end of the date I would kiss her. No ifs, ands, or buts. So as I sat at my desk, carefully crafting descriptions of necklaces hand-designed by blind nuns in exile, I plotted my maneuvers. Was it best to ask Tracy out over lunch, or in the afternoon when she'd be tired and eager for a distraction? Should I send her a cutesy email with a MacPaint caricature of our CEO in the bathtub, or should I do it face-to-face? Just when I thought I had it figured out, I looked up to find Tracy standing in front of my desk, with an awkward smile.

Tracy: Looks like it's gonna snow this weekend. Wanna go sledding in Central Park?

Me: Wha...uh...oh...yeah? Yeah! Of course I do. Sounds fun!

And there it was! She asked me out! And what could be cuter and sweeter and more romantic than a lovely sledding date? It was far better than anything I could've crafted myself–playful and fun, while still rich with datey potential. She would zip down a hill, then stumble on her way back up. I would rush to help her, and we would fall into a tender embrace. I'll take two tickets to Smooch City, please. Or how about a jovial little snowball fight? That's something people do, right? We would toss snowballs at each other, then break into hysterics when we accidentally hit a passerby. She would laugh, then I would laugh, then it would be clear to us both how perfect we were for each other. And then, of course, we'd fuck! How delightful. I knew right then that I was right about Tracy all along. One in a million, that girl was!

I arrived at Central Park on Sunday while the snow was still falling. Kids were everywhere, the ground was covered in fresh powder–it was the kind of date scenario that would've given Norman Rockwell an erection. I saw Tracy standing atop one of the big hills, looking adorable as she scoped out the best place to sled. It was so perfect that I considered running to her and kissing her right then and there, ending the drama and allowing us to have the perfect afternoon together as a couple. As I approached, however, I noticed that she appeared to be talking to someone. A guy our age, who looked to be pointing out the best angles for top velocity. I waved to Tracy, and both she and her companion waved back. Hmm, it appeared that Tracy had brought a friend.

His name was Kyle, and he certainly had a flair for sledding. He attacked the hill, taking several running strides before launching onto his rubber innertube, zipping dangerously close to five different kids' heads. He sled in blue jeans, sneakers, and an apparently ironic Member's Only jacket. He was a good guy, Kyle, if a little aggressive in the hipster department. Although his presence meant I would have to work a little harder to find a moment to sneak a kiss from Tracy, it was fine to have another along for the snow day fun. Perhaps he could be our first couple friend!

We took turns sliding down the hill on our one innertube. The sledding was fun, but I most looked forward to Kyle's turn on the slopes, so I could remain up high with Tracy and throw some kindling on the chemistry fire. It was a little awkward, she seemed kinda distracted, but I was sure it was just the romantic tension getting to her. After all, several months of flirtation had lead up to this one day. As it was nearing the end of the afternoon, Kyle stomped up the hill and handed me the innertube.

Kyle: One last ride down hell mountain, good man?

That was how Kyle talked. Typical Kyle, am I right? I took the sled and jumped down the hill, but halfway down I hit a vicious patch of ice. The tube spun wildly, and then flipped over, flinging me out into the snow. It hurt like hell, but I made sure to get up with a smile, so I could impress Tracy with my indomitable spirit, in case she was watching. When I looked back up to the hill however, it was clear that I didn't have to worry about Tracy judging my awkward fall. There was no way she could have seen it, for at that particular moment, Tracy was kissing the living shit out of her pal Kyle.

After that, I did what any self-respecting man would do: I told the lovebirds that I wasn't feeling well, and I went home. A few days later, I confronted Tracy about the situation and she apologized for not telling my about Kyle, who she'd been dating for...wait for it...the last six months. I told her I understood, that it can be hard to find just the right way to bring up your boyfriend to the other guy you were on a date with. It was clear that Tracy did in fact like me, but wasn't sure in exactly what way, and had gotten herself into a situation far more complicated than she could handle. I was angry, she grew uncomfortable around me, and when she announced she was moving to California a few months later, I bid her adieu.

Is Internet dating better than traditional dating? I haven't the slightest idea. No matter what platform you're using, dating still involves people—whether you meet them on the computer, in a coffee shop, or at the desk next to yours at the most ridiculous Internet company on Earth. People, sometimes, let you down. At least when you meet them online, you know they're actually single and hoping to date. OK, sometimes you don't know that. But the point is, dating can be a disaster no matter how you do it, so you might as well go with what makes you comfortable. And for me, crafting the perfect email, planning what I'm gonna say when we meet, and discovering whether this girl is going to be The One, or just another great story to share with you folks, well, that's what workse. For better or for worse, it's what makes me comfortable. If you're the same way, maybe I'll see you online sometime. Good luck.

ABOUT THE AUTHOR

Brian Donovan has written for *Late Night with Jimmy Fallon, National Public Radio*, and, most recently, ABC's *The Neighbors*. His work has also appeared on Chapelle's Show, Funny or Die, and Off Broadway in New York City. His most recent book "Chunk" is currently being developed for television by ABC.

Made in the USA
Charleston, SC
11 March 2016